FROM ROSE BOWL TO RASHI

A UNIQUE JOURNEY TO ORTHODOX JUDAISM

EMUNAH VERED MURRAY

FROMROSEBOWLTORASHI.COM

This book is dedicated to our children,
our most precious gifts from Hashem:

Calvin Jr.
Brandon
Andrew
Corey
Isaiah
Hannah

May they go from strength to strength!

In loving memory of our dear parents:

Joan Carol Murray
October 24, 1935 – April 22, 2009

Leon Murray
December 1, 1935 – September 22, 1991

Nancy Ann Leugers
June 29, 1938 – March 22, 2014

Gerald Allen Weaver
August 18, 1936 – September 25, 2000

TABLE OF CONTENTS

APPROBATIONS

Yosef and Emunah Murray came to our Kehilla having invested ten years into researching and learning about Judaism and its responsibilities and beauty. While their story is fascinating, and sure to be an example for those finding their faith, their commitment to the community and generosity is something they have humbly left out of the story.

This self-effacing couple actively pursued opportunities to give of their time and resources to the community from the moment they moved in. Yosef brought a true sense of working as a team to the leadership of our community, something highly valuable in a small Jewish town. Emunah writes of how she was welcomed by the Columbus community, and while that is true, she also wasted no time in becoming a contributing member of her social and congregational circles.

This speaks to the Murray's dedication as well as the maturity that they brought with them, as they came with grown children and having dedicated so many years of their lives to patiently studying and taking the steps necessary to fully acclimate to an entirely new way of life.

I can only wish Yosef and Emunah continued Hatzlacha in growing in Torah and Mitzvos, coming ever closer to Hashem. May they see success in all of their endeavors, as this is a couple that understands that their journey continues until 120, in good health.

RABBI CHAIM YOSEF ACKERMAN

On Chol Hamoed Sukkot a few years ago, we were in our sukkah, waiting for a couple who was visiting from Ohio. They were interested in life in Israel with the possibility of making aliyah sometime in the future. We made aliyah in 2010 and were good resources for them.

We looked up and the Murrays stood at the entrance of our sukkah. They not only entered our temporary abode, but also our hearts and lives. That's the long and short of it. And we mean that literally. There stood Yosef Murray, very tall, nearly filling the entry way. With him was petite Emunah.

We imagined spending an hour together, schmoozing, answering questions, hearing about their relatively recent Orthodox Jewish lives, talking about our children, our goals as observant Jews, what daily life is like in Eretz Yisrael, and, of course, probe any possibility that we know people in common.

Yosef and Emunah moved and inspired us with their story and with their sincerity and resilience, given what they had to go through to get to where they were. The more we talked, laughed and shared, the more we clicked. What we expected to be an hour-long chat turned into an afternoon of friendship.

We took them around the neighborhood, dropped them off to visit another couple and went to have a meal at the local mall. We anxiously awaited their next visit, and before long, Emunah informed us that indeed, aliyah was in her plans. She was coming to live in our neighborhood, and Yosef would seriously consider joining her as often as possible, hopefully with an eye towards aliyah as well. Everything in its own time.

Emunah made friends immediately. That's no surprise if you know her and her perky, inviting personality. She is thirsty for all Israel has to offer and she lets you know her soul has permanent residence in the Holy Land. She and Yosef are serious, growing, intelligent and uncompromising Jews. And when Yosef is here with Emunah, their love for each other and joy with each other knows no bounds.

II

It takes people in our neighborhood and beyond a nanosecond to sniff out that Yosef Murray is a football legend. Kids crowd around him and can't get enough of him. He surely has lots to offer youth as an oleh. Both Emunah and Yosef continue to be shining examples of sheer willpower to be in the vineyard of Hashem and to come closer to Him and His people on a daily basis. We love them and consider them dear friends.

May the Almighty continue to bless them with success in their journey, may their children and grandchildren be inspired by these angels in their family, and may Yosef and Emunah Murray eventually live their ultimate dream.

RABBI ELAN & DR. RIVKAH LAMBERT ADLER

Dear Emunah and Yosef,

I am sorry that I didn't write sooner. I have tried to put my thoughts in chronologic order, to no avail. Simply, I have been involved with a Beth Din for gerus for almost 38 years. I have seen many candidates come and go.

All those who apply appear sincere and most want to become Jewish for the right reasons. Most impress me by their sincerity. However, what separates a candidate from true Ger (convert) is the staying power and sincere commitment for the long haul. Being Jewish requires not only faith but consistent actions. The difference is one's actions. For only they reveal true commitment and belief.

In Emunah and Yosef's case, they weren't just sincere and committed. They were a wholesome couple who spent their lives assisting others. They were spiritual leaders in their community. They lacked nothing except for finding Truth.

Theirs is a story not just of love, commitment and faith – their story is an inspiration. For us, for their community, and for all who will find out about their fascinating and genuine pursuit of G-d and G-d's ways. I thank the Murrays for allowing me to help them, even in a small way. For their journey accomplishes the spiritual journey we all wish we could follow. Chazak!

RABBI CHAIM MOSHE BERGSTEIN
Council of Orthodox Rabbis of Greater Detroit

With joy in my heart, I am privileged to recommend a most inspiring book entitled, *From Rose Bowl to Rashi*, by my dear friends Emunah and Yosef Murray. The Murrays are an extraordinary couple whose journey to observant Judaism is a moving story of love, dedication and character development. Yosef (born Calvin) took the lessons of the Big Ten and the NFL to serving Hashem, showing that he is a true champion whether on the field or off. Emunah (born Jeri), bears the name that describes her best. This book shows how Torah and emuna are the way to a sweet life, while providing a lovely insight into what makes people truly great.

May Hashem bless the Murray family with the best of material and spiritual abundance, and much success with this book. I urge everyone to read it.

With Blessings,

RABBI ELIEZER RAPHAEL (LAZER) BRODY
Mashpia Ruchni – Spiritual Dean
Chut Shel Chessed Yeshiva and Breslev Israel

Dear Yosef and Emunah,

I feel privileged to have been given the opportunity to preview your wonderful book, "From Rose Bowl to Rashi." I found it to be refreshing and inspiring. To travel with you in your pursuit of truth is exciting. I can't imagine the patience and fortitude necessary to navigate your transition, culminating in your conversion process. Kol Hakavod!

Every journey involves not only a destination, but also a point of departure. It took, and takes, a great deal of courage to leave behind, or modify, so many relationships that were an essential part of your lives. But when you are sincerely seeking truth, nothing can divert you from your mission. You set a good example for Jews from birth - to take Judaism seriously, and joyfully. Many of us have no idea how fortunate we are. You serve as both students and teachers.

Two thoughts about the title: Firstly, the Rose Bowl is usually once in a lifetime – Rashi is forever! Secondly, Emunah, your chosen middle name, Vered, means Rose. You are, therefore, embedded in the title of your own book, and your Rose should continue to blossom for many years to come.

May you both continue to grow from strength to strength, and be a source of inspiration for all of us. It is both a pleasure and a privilege to be part of your lives. With blessings for true success in all that you do,

Your Friend,

RABBI CHAIM CAPLAND
The Torah Center

As is the case for many people, I have been blessed to meet extraordinary people on my journey. Yosef and Emunah are no exception. I have the pleasure of knowing them both.

I watched the 1980 Rose Bowl game in real time, and then recently reviewed it on YouTube. In that game, The Ohio State team was winning in the fourth quarter on the legs of Calvin "In A Hurry" Murray. With only minutes left, Calvin suffered a concussion, and The OSU Buckeyes' hopes fell along with him on the field.

Yosef "In A Hurry" Murray always works to be the best at what he does, including sports, family, work, giving guidance to at-risk teens, and spiritual growth. The spiritual journey that he and Emunah took required great personal sacrifices of family, friends and finances. They could not be deterred from finding the truth. Christianity's loss is our gain.

The journey for a convert is one of finding spiritual truth, discovering your true name and mission, and your true fit in the world. We are blessed that Yosef and Emunah are helping carry the football for the Jewish people to the goal of world peace. Go Murrays, go!

AVRAHAM (JAMES) EASTMAN
(US Army Major, RET)
Former Head Coach of the Judean Rebels of the Israel Football League | Head Coach of the Petach Tikvah (Israel) Troopers

Ki ner mitzvah v'Torah ohr,
"The mitzvah is a lamp and Torah is the light"
(Proverbs 6:23)

The "Torah" is the Jewish word for the Law or Bible and this word is rooted in the word for light -Ohr. In my football days as a fullback, the coaches would instill in us the concept of running toward the light, i.e. find an opening and run as fast as you can toward the light to reach the goal. Yosef has learned this teaching well in his spiritual quest as he has made a beeline toward the light--Torah and his Beshert, Emunah, with her strong faith, drive and persistence has shown herself worthy to be his lamp as they travel together the path of Torah.

Their mutual goal has been to learn, teach and do what they have learned on their journey. Their story in their own words has been one of exceptional inspiration. Reading their story brings a sense of awe to those who read it. I look forward to hearing and seeing the continual progress they make as they conquer their world through their exceptional faith and as they strive toward Truth.

RABBI YAKOV GOLDBERG
Breslov Judaic Center

Several years ago, I was privileged to meet Emunah Murray and her daughter Hannah, when they came to Israel to volunteer service for the IDF. Emunah related that she and her husband, Yosef, were in the process of converting to Judaism. I was very impressed when I met Emunah and Hannah. When they returned home to Columbus, Ohio we maintained contact daily.

It has always been a privilege for me to meet converts from around the world for the past twenty years. However, in all honesty, when I met Emunah I was really impressed by her sincere commitment to Judaism. A year later, once again I was privileged to meet Emunah and her husband, Yosef, when they came to Israel for the high holidays. I was exceedingly impressed with this couple.

When Emunah told me she was writing a book about hers and Yosef's journey to Judaism, I was very excited. To young people and older people, I highly recommend this book.

It will give you an understanding of a husband and wife team through their ups and downs as they came to the belief in the one and only God. Their life story is inspiring and will encourage you in your struggles to strive for the Truth and trust in God. From Rose Bowl to Rashi, is the story of a team effort of two determined individuals to serve Hashem with all their heart and soul. As Shlomo Hamelech says in Mishlei (Proverbs) 13:20, "He who walks with the wise will grow wise." I have personally been inspired by the life and love of this couple.

AHUVAH GRAY
Author

In the Spring of 2009 I had the privilege of serving as the Headmaster of the Columbus Torah Academy. CTA, as the school is called, is an Orthodox Jewish day school that has served the Jewish community of Columbus, Ohio for more than fifty years. One beautiful sunny day, my secretary buzzed me to say that a non-Jewish family had come to visit the school and they wished to meet with me about enrolling their daughter. That is how I met Calvin and Jeri Murray (as they were then known) for the first time. It would be a profound understatement to say that I had never met individuals like Calvin and Jeri before.

After taking my guests on a tour of the school, I invited them to my office for a chat. I asked them why they were interested in sending their child to a Jewish school. The story they shared with me that day astounded and touched me. It was a story of two people who were on a mission to find the truth and who would not let anything stand in their way. Their level of commitment and dedication to find Hashem inspired me then and continues to inspire and move me to this day. It will inspire you, too.

Calvin and Jeri pursued their quest and fulfilled their dream of becoming authentic, Torah-observant Jews. Their new Hebrew names, Yosef and Emunah, suit them perfectly. It has been a great honor and pleasure for my family to sit at Yosef's and Emunah's Shabbat table enjoying Emunah's delicious cooking and Yosef's thoughts on the Parasha.

These two extraordinary people are as down-to-earth as can be. They are completely unassuming and modest about their remarkable spiritual accomplishments.

They appear unaware of the fact that they are walking in the footsteps of Yitro, Tziporah, Ruth and the other great heroes throughout Jewish history who made a conscious choice to join Am Yisroel and add ("Yosef" means add) their wisdom and pure, simple faith ("Emunah" means faith) and strength to our people.

May Hashem continue to bless Yosef and Emunah Murray with all good things and may Yosef and Emunah continue to grow in Torah, Mitzvot and closeness to Hashem.

RABBI ZVI KAHN
Head of School
Hebrew Academy (RASG)

Maimonides is his Mishne Torah uses a perplexing phrase — "When a convert, converts." This seems strange because if a convert is already Jewish, then why is the process of conversion required? It should have said when a non-Jew becomes Jewish. The Rebbe of blessed memory explains that a convert always possessed a lost Jewish soul but in order to rediscover that soul, the process of conversion needed to be completed.

Yosef and Emunah's Jewishness was always apparent in their lives. So while they always had a Jewish soul, they needed a process to bring it out. Even when they weren't Jewish, their lives always represented Jewish values.

Yosef's biblical namesake, Joseph, is appropriate because it represents someone who never became a victim to his tortuous circumstance. Rather, he overcame his many challenges and ended up saving the world from hunger. It is no wonder why our Yosef, in 1979, was the last running back at The Ohio State University to wear a tear away football jersey. He never gave up and endured to the end because failure was not an option.

The Hebrew word, emunah, means faith. When a person has true emunah in their Creator, then no force can hold them back from crossing into the end zone and completing their mission. Our Emunah is a devoted shining example of someone who takes her Yiddishkeit very seriously.

When Maimonides said "When a convert, converts," I know he had our Yosef and Emunah in mind. To know the Murrays is to love the Murrays, for they are found Jewish souls.

RABBI AREYAH KALTMANN
The Lori Schottenstein Chabad Center

FORWARD

BY YERACHMIEL HENIG

"That was beautiful. *I've heard your voice before!*"

I considered the man's beaming face to gauge how much he meant that compliment.

The Friday before, I had finished work too late at the Chabad Center to drive home to Detroit before sundown and was consequently stuck in New Albany, Ohio, for Shabbat. Almost as a last resort (really because no one else wanted to do it), the rabbi had asked me to lead services.

"Where else have you heard me lead services? This is my first time here."

"In a dream." *He was sincere.*

And, that is how I was introduced to Calvin – now appropriately named Yosef, and his living, technicolor dreams.

He was on a journey, he said, as I further probed this powerfully-built former football star with the deep wisdom in his eyes – together with his wife, Jeri. The two had been questing for Truth and hadn't yet found it to any satisfying degree in the religions and cultures they had previously explored. Orthodox Judaism, on the other hand, seemed right.

By the time I met them, Calvin and Jeri had already decided to become Jews. I was immediately intrigued to understand why it was so important for them. What motivated this rampant desire for which they seemed willing to risk instability and interfamilial strife, giving up friends and comforts, aside from all the regular inconveniences of being Orthodox Jewish?

(Have you ever checked out the non-kosher meat department in the supermarket by mistake? Talk about your "sticker-shock"!)

I probed further. Did they realize that – unlike other religions which teach that "infidels" are condemned to Hell – Judaism does not require a gentile to convert, only to lead a righteous life in accordance with the Noachide Laws, that essentially encapsulate what would have once been commonly known as "decency"? That, plus the recognition of G-d as the Creator and Provider, and you're "golden"!

Calvin and Jeri, who had by now sat down with me for after-service refreshments, would have none of that.

"We've already been told this," said Jeri, "and I know you're supposed to discourage prospective converts in the initial stages, to weed out the insincere. But, we've already made up our minds. We seek a closeness to Hashem (I was touched by the way she pronounced that Name with such love and feeling) that can only be realized as part of His People."

Who was I to argue?

Well, you know what happens when you throw an interesting black man into a mix of white Jews at a *kiddush* table? In no time at all, your exclusive interview with him is over!

Then, when the crazy Buckeye fans discovered who this Calvin Murray really is, with his longstanding achievement record for THE TEAM, I was sure I'd never get a chance to catch his attention again.

I was wrong. Calvin was not distracted by the adulation. He and Jeri seemed to sense that they had much more to talk to me about. They seemed to trust that I was knowledgeable in Judaism and would give them honest answers in areas where others might have been evasive.

So, our conversation resumed, and I'm blessed to say, it continues to this day.

Before leaving him alone finally, so he could talk to me, one of Calvin's fans at the table asked him for a business card, to be in touch. This fan was obviously not observant, as is often the case with many attendees at a Chabad kiddush, where all are warmly welcomed and made to feel like "life members."

Calvin leaned over to the young man, "If I give you a card, you will carry it home, right?"

"Yes," said the fan.

"Well, then I can't give it to you," said Calvin, "because I'll be causing you to violate the Shabbat."

"Welcome home, my brother, welcome home," I thought.

PRELIMINARY REMARKS

Hashem is a Hebrew term for G-d. Literally, it means "The Name." The third of the Ten Commandments prohibit us from saying G-d's name in vain. Out of reverence and to be extra scrupulous about not using G-d's name in vain, Hashem often will be used in place of the word "G-d." In various places Hebrew calendar dates will be used. Our given names of Calvin and Jeri will be used when referring to pre-conversion, and our Hebrew names, Yosef and Emunah thereafter. Additionally, for our readers who may be unfamiliar with Hebrew words, a glossary is provided at the back of this book.

The name Rashi is synonymous with Judaism. Rabbi Shlomo Yitzchaki, commonly known by the acronym Rashi (RAbbi SHlomo Itzhaki), was a medieval French rabbi and author of a commentary on the *Tanakh* (the Hebrew Bible). He is known for his ability to present the basic meaning of the text in a succinct, plain and simple fashion. The study of the Hebrew Bible using the Rashi commentary appeals to both scholarly and beginning students. Rashi beautifully explains the Hebrew text with an approach enabling most people to understand the meaning. Thus, when we began in earnest to study the Tanakh, we found it very helpful to look to and study Rashi's commentary to gain a better understanding of the Hebrew text. We thought it appropriate to use his name in the title of our book, since his commentary was instrumental in our study and understanding of the Hebrew Bible. Located on the front cover of our book is Rashi text, which is found in every *Chumash* (the Five Books of Moses).

Although Emunah authored this book, Yosef was involved with providing the history of his early years and football career. It is our story, as told by Emunah, with Yosef's input.

We hope our story is one of inspiration. This book is for Jews, non-Jews, Christians, questioning Christians, sports/football fans, or anyone else interested in life lessons learned from rising through the ranks, from pee-wee football to the pros, journeying through different realms of spirituality, and being true to your heart and passions, sometimes at great personal cost.

PREFACE

"Your people are my people; your G-d is my G-d."
(Ruth 1:16)

Many people ask, "What made you want to convert to Orthodox Judaism?" This is a valid question, but one whose answer is difficult to provide with a few simple remarks. Sometimes words just don't do justice to what you feel in your heart and soul. For us, the process resembled a giant spiritual jigsaw puzzle with various pieces fitting together over a decade of intense searching and study. There was not one particular event or nugget of Scripture that convinced us; rather, we would describe it as a journey, a deeply spiritual journey, and one which we have treasured through every stage. This is not to say that the path has not sometimes been difficult and remains so to date. Yosef describes it as his soul being driven and feeling unable to find rest. There was no stopping and no rest. Nothing satisfied this drive but to continue our spiritual quest back to Mount Sinai. It is akin to a spiritual GPS. Hashem programmed the destination, and down the path we traveled. As is said about attaining *emunah* (faith in G-d), when first exposed to Judaism, it was like a spark ignited that grew into a raging flame. Nothing could extinguish this flame, and the only choice for us was to move closer to the Torah and Judaism. Emunah said, "I felt like my soul has been roaming, and now it can finally rest, having reached home."

According to the Talmud (*Shavuot* 39a), the souls of all converts were actually present at Mount Sinai when the Torah was given. In *Devarim* (Deuteronomy) 29:13, the Torah states, "Not with you alone do I seal this covenant, but with whoever is here, standing with us today before the Almighty our G-d, and with whoever is not here with us today."

The Talmud states that this refers to converts who would join the Jewish people in the future. There is a *Midrash* (commentary on the Bible) which states that G-d, before offering the Torah to the Jews at Mt. Sinai, offered it to all the other nations. None of them were willing to accept the rules and regulations as a nation, but among them were individuals who were willing to accept the Torah. We feel like we were of those souls who waved frantically to G-d and said, "Me! Me!" These converts wanted to express their willingness to accept the Torah and be part of the Jewish nation. The Midrash also states that when G-d gave the Torah to His people at Mt. Sinai, the souls of the converts were also present, those who so eagerly wanted to accept the Torah as their own. This Midrash really resonates with us, and maybe this explains being drawn like a magnet to the Torah and Judaism. Hasidic thought reinforces the teaching that all righteous converts were at Mt. Sinai with every other Jew, born and unborn.

We are so very grateful that Hashem made provision in His Word for people like us. He foresaw that there would be people who loved *Shabbos* (Shabbat/Jewish Sabbath) and the Covenant, as it states in Isaiah 56:6-7, "Even them will I bring to My holy mountain and make them joyful in My house of prayer." There are many instructions in the Torah concerning how to treat converts, and when we read these, we always smile, knowing that our Father in Heaven wrote special instructions just for us.

This seems to be a plausible explanation as to why we were absolutely driven and propelled toward Judaism. We had an unquenchable thirst for intimacy with Hashem and connection to the Jewish people. We would not be at peace until the day of our conversion when we finally arrived "home." After visiting Israel for the first time in 2007, Emunah felt a strong connection to the Land of Israel. That connection would come a bit later for Yosef.

Although we no longer believe Christianity to be the proper path for Jews, Yosef feels it could be a possible pathway to the Creator for non-jews, Emunah thinks that it is not appropriate for anyone, even non-Jews.

Both Yosef and Emunah recommend exploration of the Noahide Laws, seven laws considered by Rabbinic tradition as the minimal moral duties required by the Bible on all people. The writings of Rabbi Tovia Singer are an excellent starting point for this research. We do not judge or condemn our friends and family who are still practicing Christianity. In fact, we are grateful to Christianity as well as to the people we met in the framework of messianic Judaism because we understand that this was a bridge, one that we needed to cross to arrive where we are today. This is the path Hashem laid out for us, and we learned many valuable lessons, lessons that enabled us to reach our destination as Torah Jews.

INTRODUCTION

Two souls, born six weeks apart in 1958 in different regions of the United States, became husband and wife at age 33, raised six children and ultimately became Orthodox Jews at age 55. What follows is our story, the story of our incredible spiritual journey, and the details of why and how we made it to our destination as Torah Jews.

Conversion to Orthodox Judaism is a wonderful, transformative experience, and it is also the hardest decision we have made in our lives. Conversion to Judaism undoubtedly involves faith – but it is much more than that. You are not just adopting a new faith. You are adopting a people, a land, the Torah, and a holy tongue.

Being a Torah Jew affects *every* area of your life – what you eat, what you wear, where you live, the relationship between spouses, education for children, articulating with a new vocabulary, and a myriad of other areas. Conversion involves not just a belief system; more importantly, it means integrating those beliefs into a lifestyle. It is not just a religion, but a way of life that truly governs every aspect of your existence: from waking in the morning to going to bed at night, from before birth until after death, and every moment in between. The far-reaching effects of converting to Judaism are not to be taken lightly, especially when children are involved. It takes courage and strength of character to embark on religious conversion. It is not for the timid or faint of heart. One of our rabbis on the *Beis Din* (Rabbinical Court) told us that very few candidates continue to the final step of immersion in the *mikveh* (ritual bath), due to the immense difficulties and sacrifices necessary to reach that point.

You must possess the fortitude to withstand rejection from your family, friends, and coworkers. We have heard unfortunate stories where family and personal relationships were totally severed; fortunately, we had only a few friends who chose not to continue our friendship. Overall, we feel our children, siblings, friends, and parents have for the most part been supportive or, at the very least, neutral. Yosef's family called him "Calvin the Jew," long before we converted, as they would always see him praying *Shacharis* (morning prayers), *Mincha* (afternoon prayers), and *Maariv* (evening prayers) when he would visit them in New Jersey. Yosef's family was curious but not combative. Emunah, having not been raised in a religious home, did not get push-back from family. Most of our family members are respectful of our beliefs and lifestyle. They accept the fact that we bring our own food to family gatherings and don't schedule activities on *Shabbos* (the Sabbath) and *Yom Tov* (Jewish holy day). These lifestyle changes take time and adjustment.

As stated previously, we had some friends who chose not to continue the friendship with us. This is one of the many challenges of conversion, and sometimes saying goodbye to people is painful. However, we believe that around these challenges, we will continue to reap immeasurable rewards of a rich, satisfying and focused way of life, both in this world and for eternity.

Once the Rabbis of the Beis Din accepted us as candidates for conversion, they told us several times, "It's not a race; it's a marathon. Try to enjoy the journey." From the first time we got a taste of Judaism to the time we converted took a little over ten years. Eight years into our journey when visiting the Beis Din for the first time, we inquired as to how long the formal conversion process might take, and were told, "One to two years." Our conversion was completed in nineteen months. We had already been studying Judaism for eight years and possessed a fairly solid foundation. Truly, it *was* a marathon. Preparation for conversion is not accomplished by just reading a few books and attending *shul* (synagogue). It is not just information that you need to amass; you need to learn how to live as a Torah Jew. One of the most difficult requirements was moving from our family home into the Jewish community. This was a tremendous challenge, not only for Yosef and me, but also for our two youngest children still living at home, who had to learn about and respect our new standards.

Once we moved into the Jewish community and began to celebrate Shabbos in many homes, we were asked repeatedly to share our story. People seemed moved and inspired, and many suggested we share our story. Our hope is that this book will be first and foremost an encouragement to the Jewish community, to understand and appreciate these most precious gifts given to them by the Creator of the universe: an eternal Covenant and a relationship with Him. These are true treasures. In addition, this book is also a glimpse into the world of "Jews by choice," and the difficult path, decisions and sacrifices that are made in order to join the Covenant and *Am Yisrael* (the Nation of Israel). We hope that by sharing our joys, fears and tears, we will give guidance to those considering the path that we chose. Again, it is not an easy path, but we cannot imagine living any other way.

Although our path was fraught with difficult and sometimes painful decisions as well as a drastic change in lifestyle, we have no regrets. The outcome has, so far, been deeply fulfilling and rewarding. One of our constant prayers was that our path would be clear and obvious. Time and time again, this specific prayer was answered. We truly believe that *emes* (truth) is available and clear to those who seek. Hashem's ways are not secret; they are accessible to those who have the courage to look deeply. We are forever grateful and humbled that we have the great privilege and responsibility of joining the Jewish People and serving *HaKadosh Baruch Hu* (the Holy One, Blessed Be He).

With much gratitude to Hashem,
Emunah Vered Murray
Adar 18, 5778

CHAPTER 1

TOUCHDOWN

February 28, 2013 – 1:15 p.m.

"Jeri! I'm so excited for you. This is the culmination of your entire life. It's happening. It's the greatest touchdown ever. Only good news. Lots of love. Lots of *brachos*. Tell Calvin that Abraham, Isaac and Jacob are rooting him on to the victory. It's touchdown at its best!"

This message of congratulations and encouragement from Rabbi Areyah Kaltmann of The Lori Schottenstein Chabad Center was left on my voice mail while Calvin and I were at the mikveh for our conversion.

Maybe this isn't the kind of touchdown you expected to read about when you picked up this book; maybe you were expecting a football story. There is plenty of that to come, but this story is really about the ten-year journey that culminated in a touchdown of life-changing proportions: immersing in the mikveh in Southfield, Michigan and adopting our new identities as Jews.

That 18th day of Adar 5773 (2013) was a day for which we had extensively prepared. Our conversion could not have happened on a more auspicious date on the Hebrew calendar. Adar is the month associated with increased joy and happiness. Eighteen is the value of the Hebrew letters *chet* and *yud*, which together spell the word *chai*, life. Since we were embarking on a new life, so to speak, it seemed meaningful and appropriate that this event occurred on the 18th of Adar. We are not at all surprised that Hashem chose this date for our life-changing experience of becoming Jewish.

CHAPTER 2

CALVIN MURRAY'S STORY
(AS TOLD BY HIM)

I was born Leon Calvin Murray on October 18, 1958 and grew up in Woodbine, New Jersey, which is a borough in Cape May County. A rural area, surrounded by forest, Woodbine was founded in 1891 as a settlement for Eastern European Jews by the wealthy German philanthropist, Baron Maurice de Hirsch. In the interest of providing persecuted Russian Jews a better lot in life, he purchased land and established a fund to assist their immigration to America. The immigrants transformed Woodbine, sometimes referred to as the Jewish Colony, into an agricultural community.

When I was young, the town consisted of predominately Jewish, African-American, and Puerto Rican families; white Protestant and Catholic families were in the minority. Growing up in a town with different cultures and different races afforded me the valuable opportunity to understand people in a broader perspective, and to be able to relate to and get along with many different kinds of people. These early experiences served me well later in my chosen career working with at-risk youth of various backgrounds. I find it interesting to reflect that I grew up in a town made up mostly of African Americans and Jews, since I would embrace these identities together later in life.

I am the oldest of five children, having three brothers, Glen, Jeffrey and Jerry, and one sister, Donna. I had the great fortune of growing up in close proximity to my extended family, many of whom lived on or near the 25-acre plot of land purchased by my grandfather. The adults fondly called it Murrayville because so many kids in the family grew up on that property –

2

in fact, twenty-two children were raised there. I was never lonely, having so many siblings and cousins with whom to play.

My parents' names were Leon and Carol Murray. My father's parents, Jeff and Ophelia Murray, lived next door. My mother's parents, Roosevelt and Annabelle Archie, were only fifteen miles away in the little town of Leesburg, New Jersey. Both of my parents came from stable homes with structure steeped in family values. These were passed to us in the day-to-day interactions rather than in isolated moments. We were taught to be responsible, attentive, thoughtful, open-minded, and virtuous members of our community.

My father was a successful entrepreneur, running his own trucking business, and there were a number of other family businesses where we kids helped out during our youth. Through these businesses, my dad and other family leaders instilled a strong work ethic in me and my siblings. Whether it was taking care of animals or refuse collection, we worked hard and realized the importance of contributing to the success of our family. That foundation resulted in thriving and long-term careers for myself and my siblings. Hard work, family dedication and respect for elders were important lessons taught in my family.

Dad also felt it was important for his children to appreciate what America has to offer by seeing new places. Over the years, he packed us into a 33-foot motor home for many treks around the country. We ventured to Mt. Rushmore, Texas, California, Florida, the Carolinas, Tennessee, Ohio, and many other sites. The high school I attended helped me expand my travels beyond the national borders by sponsoring European trips to Austria, Germany, England, Scotland, Wales, and Switzerland. My parents felt it was important for us to see what life was like in other countries and to further realize the privilege of living in America. This exposure developed a deep interest in and admiration of other cultures.

Holidays were celebrated in both their religious and commercial aspects, and Thanksgiving always stood out for the sheer size of the gathering. My mom came from a family of 16 children and one of my aunts had eight

3

kids. All told, there were between 75-100 people breaking bread together to acknowledge the blessings of the year and the importance of family. With a crowd that large, celebrating in a home was not possible, and we rented the VFW or some other hall for our gatherings. Eating meals as a family fosters a strong bond and, without ever stating it as a rule, Mom and Dad required this on a daily basis. Holiday meals with the large, extended family only enhanced that bond. This particular holiday was one that all the kids looked forward to every year.

In the midst of this Jewish Colony called Woodbine, the Murray family were devout Baptists, and it was ingrained in us from an early age that G-d was central to our lives. Many of my family members held important roles as teachers, deacons, and elders in the church, and I participated in Sunday school, church camps, Vacation Bible School, and even preached my first sermon when I was fourteen years old! Who knew this would be the beginning of my public speaking career?

One night, my aunts took me to a tent revival, a service conducted in the summer by traveling evangelist ministers under a large tent. The evangelist lined up all the participants in a row and said, "Something special is going to happen to somebody here." I closed my eyes and saw a *tallis* (a shawl worn by Jewish men during morning prayers) with the *tzitzis* (the fringes on the tallis) blowing in the wind. I reached out and grabbed ahold of it but, as I had never seen a tallis, had no idea what it meant at that particular time. In retrospect, I believe that this was a seed planted in me, a Jewish ritual that would take on meaning later in life.

Discussing Bible stories was a frequent activity in our family. Grandma Archie was known as a "prayer warrior," and she always told us children to read Psalm 91. I could never have predicted that years later I would be reciting that exact Psalm every day in Shacharis. I remember her often going upstairs in her house and saying over her shoulder, "I'm going to talk to G-d." She would enter what she called her prayer closet for those private conversations with her Creator.

My parents are my heroes. My mother sacrificed so much for us kids and protected us in ways I did not understand until I was an adult. My father taught me important lessons on how to make a contribution to the world, how to treat and interact with people, and how to have honest business dealings. The foundation they laid had a profound influence on me, affecting how I managed my careers and raised my family.

When it was time for high school, I found myself traveling 26 miles each way by bus to Millville High, a large and predominately white school. Several surrounding boroughs and townships sent their high school students to Millville as part of a sending/receiving relationship. While it was a hardship to spend so much time on the bus every day, the school afforded me the opportunity for better academics and college preparation.

As my circle of influencers widened beyond my parents and family, I was blessed to have a number of formidable role models, particularly in the area of sports. One especially notable mentor was my ninth-grade football coach, Coach Caldwell. Before teaching me the first play, he said to me, "Cal, what are your goals?" I remember looking at him with a blank stare, thinking, "You mean besides getting a touchdown?" I had never given much thought to goals, and I honestly did not know how to answer his question. He must have sensed my confusion because he clarified with, "What do you want to do with your life? Where do you want to go? Who do you want to be?"

Heavy questions for a ninth grader. At that age I didn't have any concept of how you decide such things, or how to begin to make it happen. Coach Caldwell pushed me to answer these questions and then told me to put my goals in writing. I wrote down that I wanted to:

Play for The Ohio State Buckeyes.

Play for the Philadelphia Eagles.

Work with kids.

This first experience with goal-setting was an important lesson I carried with me in raising my own children and in my career working with at-risk and disadvantaged youth.

Coach Wright, another high school football coach, served as my spiritual mentor by introducing me to the Fellowship of Christian Athletes

(FCA), an organization which I was involved with throughout my high school, college, and NFL days. Today, high school sports coaches are discouraged from introducing students to religious organizations, but in my youth, this was not in the least unusual. FCA allowed students a forum to get together to share their faith and encourage one another. As such, FCA was one of my spiritual anchors in high school and beyond.

Even though I was already playing pee-wee football at age eight, I seriously began to develop my talent in ninth grade. In my freshman year, I ran for 2,000 yards and scored 16 touchdowns in just six games. (For those not well-versed in football, if a player runs for 100 yards in any one game, he has had an exceptional game. If a player gains 2,000 yards in six games, this equals over 300 yards per game, which is a rare occurrence.) Coach Caldwell retired my jersey, number 32, for one year, meaning that no one else could use that number for a year. Retiring a player's jersey is a way of honoring and acknowledging that player's skill, accomplishments and contributions. This truly bolstered my self-esteem. He praised me by saying he knew he would never coach another player like me. I remembered those words well into my college and professional career and always gave a hundred percent to live up to the faith he had in me.

My parents attended all of my athletic events. I can't remember them ever missing even one. Not only did I have parental support, but extended family would come out to watch and support me as well. It was exciting for the little town of Woodbine; and it was exciting for me. After Jeri and I were married and had our own family, our five sons and daughter were involved in various sports, and when they played a team whose stands were empty, I would ache deeply for those athletes. I knew what it meant to have parental support. Inspired by the loving support of my own parents, I attended all of my kids' athletic events and other school activities.

I began to receive letters from colleges in earnest during my junior year in high school. This was the year that Millville was in the playoffs and proceeded to win the championship, the first ever for Millville. Coached by Tony Surace, our team was considered underdogs that year despite the fact

6

that we had a perfect record of 11-0. But we made history by defeating the opposing team predicted to win. One of my teammates, Anthony "Bubba" Green, was later drafted by the Baltimore Colts. It's amazing that two of us from the tiny town of Woodbine eventually went on to be picked up in the same NFL draft.

In a state championship semi-final game against Dephert, a school close to Philadelphia, I played an exceptional game that so impressed the Dephert coach that he gushed about me to an Ohio State football coach during a recruiting trip. He showed George Chaump the game film and told him, "This boy scored six touchdowns on me. I couldn't stop him! You need to consider him for your team." I wonder if Coach Chaump hadn't had this bug put in his ear by a rival coach, how would my journey have been different? Would I still have realized my goal of playing for the Buckeyes?

Shortly after that, the schools started calling. Minnesota was the first to come to Woodbine for a scouting visit, but once George Chaump and Woody Hayes from The Ohio State University came, the floodgates opened and several other colleges began to recruit me. Ara Parseegent from Notre Dame, Johnny Majors from Tennessee, and many smaller schools, began to visit and make offers.

I personally visited the University of Minnesota, Ohio State, North Carolina State, and University of Arizona campuses. I was scheduled to visit Notre Dame, but at that point had already decided to accept the offer from Ohio State. I did not think it was honest to visit Notre Dame, feeling it would have been a waste of their time and mine, so I canceled this visit. Only later did I learn that this follows a precept in Judaism that translates to "not stealing the mind." You are not supposed to go into a store you know you will not buy from because the vendor gets his hopes up unfairly.

When head coach Woody Hayes came to Millville High School, I have to admit I was a little perplexed that he talked to everyone in my family but me. I remember saying, "I'm the one who has to make the decision." But Woody said to me, "I'll deal with you later." One thing that stood out in my mind about my recruiting visit to Ohio State was that it was the only school

7

that didn't put me up in a five-star hotel. They put me in the dorm with the regular students. Coach Hayes said, "How do you know which school to choose to go to if you're not around the kids that you're going to be with? You're not going to live with me. You're going to be around these kids. And if you don't like them, then you're not going to like the school." That attitude impressed me very much. Ron Springs, one of the players, was my escort at Ohio State and took the time to show me all around the campus, and gave me a pretty good feel for what it would be like to be a student and athlete at the university.

My family was also very impressed with Woody Hayes – they still talk about that meeting some 40 years later! Once my dad realized that I had a chance to play for a major university like Ohio State, he said, "Son, you have to go." Ohio State was Dad's favorite Big-Ten team, so this was a dream come true for him as much as it was for me. He made it to every football game, no matter how far he had to travel. He said, "You can offer me a million dollars and I wouldn't trade it for this time."

While football was a central theme of my high school years, another notable event happened when I was a senior. In the midst of games and college visits and regular high school activities, some of my friends approached me and said, "Calvin, we want you to run for senior class president." One classmate joked, "We're so sure you'll win, we'll write your acceptance speech for you." This was another opportunity to put Coach Caldwell's goal-setting lessons into practical experience. With my previous experience speaking in Sunday school and church, I was comfortable standing in front of my classmates and speaking about my goals for the class. Even though my classmates' confidence in me encouraged me, I was surprised when the announcement came over the school PA system, "Cal Murray has been elected senior class president."

This was a very exciting time in my life, setting the stage for two satisfying careers. I was so privileged to be chosen to represent the interests of my fellow students as class president, and to have my choice of universities at which to continue playing football. The crowning result was speaking at my graduation ceremony in front of the other graduates and their families. I was well on my way to achieving those goals Coach Caldwell made me write down.

CHAPTER 3

GOAL #1: PLAY FOOTBALL FOR THE OHIO STATE UNIVERSITY

I did it! I had achieved my first goal on the list I composed in the 9th grade. On September 10th, 1977, I walked into Ohio Stadium, aptly nicknamed the Horseshoe after its shape, for my first game as an Ohio State Buckeye. In the locker room before the game, we could hear the dull rumble of the crowd, but it was nothing compared to the thundering roar as we ran out on the field. At that time the stadium capacity was just over 83,000; and every fan, excited to kick off the football season, was on his or her feet cheering.

Sitting in the locker room before the game, doubts started to creep into my head. I had butterflies in my stomach like I had never before experienced. I was determined to run through visualizations of myself executing the plays we had practiced for weeks leading up to this game, but I was overwhelmed. Images of me tripping and falling while running out onto the field started to compete for attention. Being a part of this team, in front of such a large group of fans, and realizing my dream, was both exhilarating and terrifying.

We won that game against the Miami Hurricanes, 10-0. I played very little that game, maybe one or two plays on special teams doing punts and kickoff returns. Being a freshman, I had low expectations, and was just thrilled to even get in the game at all. My parents were so excited just to see me run out on the field. And I was relieved that I did not trip and fall!

Adjusting to college life was much more challenging than I had anticipated. I was very fortunate to receive a full scholarship to OSU covering my tuition, housing, books, and meals. But the realization of the weight of being a college student and a Big Ten college athlete while adapting to a completely new environment, far from the close family that had surrounded me up to now, was at times crushing. I wondered from day to day how I would manage the time commitment alone.

I spent the summer after high school graduation preparing my body for the next level of football. I weighed only 150 pounds and needed to bulk up before getting on the field with the big guys. I trained by running in the sand at the beach and lifting weights. I worked hard to ensure I was prepared for the upcoming football season. I was so focused on the physical preparation that I didn't give any thought to the other aspects of leaving home, which is likely why it was a bit of a rude awakening.

Ironically, I was assigned a roommate with the same first name, Leon (although I went by Calvin my whole life so as not to be confused with my dad). Leon Ellison was a linebacker from Washington, D.C. who told me when we met that he remembered me from the recruiting weekend about a year before. I was surprised he would have taken any notice, since most guys who are attending a recruiting event are more internally focused, thinking about how they look to the coaches. He explained that he noticed that I was a religious guy, and not one who was going to be out partying and getting into trouble. He said he was looking for a roommate who would hold him accountable and help him stay focused. I realized I wanted the same, and that forged a bond that has endured for more than 40 years.

Our dorm room was located on the eighth floor of Steeb Hall. My first night there was exciting, because everyone was abuzz getting to know each other and examining the surroundings. It was also a bit lonely, since it was my first time away from home and family. Coming from a large family, I was accustomed to being around a lot of people and hearing a lot of noise, so it stands to reason that I would acclimate to dorm life quickly. Our floor was a mixture of males and females, athletes and non-athletes, from all different backgrounds. It was a challenge to tune out the distractions and get accustomed to everyone's idiosyncrasies.

It didn't take long for the personal interaction skills I had picked up during my travels across America with the family and to Europe with my school to kick in to help me make friends. While I had many friends outside the football team, I spent most of the little free time I had with a couple of fellow freshman players.

Shortly after moving into the dorm, Leon Ellison and Vince Skillings and I were disenchanted with our experience as freshman football players, tired of getting beat up during the grueling football practice, and homesick. We declared among ourselves, "We're going to take a break and go home." Vince lived near Pittsburgh; Leon was going to D.C.; I was going home to Jersey. We walked to downtown Columbus where we intended to catch a Greyhound bus to begin our respective trips home. As we passed a church where a service was in progress, we stopped, looked at each other, and decided to go inside and listen to the pastor for a few minutes. It was not long before we found ourselves on our knees praying to G-d. Soon we felt G-d had given us the strength to go back to campus and finish what we had started. And that's what we did. We walked back to campus and continued on with our mission as athletes and students.

In high school, I had worn number 32 on my jersey because that was the jersey number of my favorite professional running back, Jim Brown. But when I arrived at OSU, number 32 was already taken, so I had to decide on a new number. My dad used to take me to Dover, Delaware to watch his favorite NASCAR driver, Richard Petty, whose number was 43. I knew it would mean a lot to my dad if I chose a number that was a symbol of our special father-son time together, so 43 was my new number.

Despite the training I did over the summer and the weight I put on to prepare for the big leagues, I was quickly enlightened to the fact that I was a small fish in a big pond. I had to start over and work hard to prove myself as a running back. Most of the rookies, including me, were assigned to play on the offensive scout team whose function is to run the plays of the upcoming opponents during practices. In all likelihood, the players on this team would never see actual game time, but the scrimmage exercises with the scout team are vital to the team's game preparation.

During the first scrimmage of the season, our nose tackle came flying over the center and knocked me flat on my backside. As he held out his hand to help me up with a grin on his face, he said, "Welcome to the Big Ten." It was certainly an eye-opener for me, and I realized I would need to pick up my pace and work much harder. Nothing would be handed to me. It was a very humbling experience to go from being a superstar starter in high school to being an unknown at Ohio State.

My freshman season culminated in an invitation to play the University of Alabama Crimson Tide, coached by Bear Bryant, in the Sugar Bowl hosted in New Orleans. My entire team was flown to New Orleans two-and-a-half weeks prior to the game as Coach Hayes wanted to get the team out of the cold and acclimated to the warmer climate prior to the game. Woody was a historian, and he made it seem like this matchup was a re-enactment of the Civil War. He would say, "Those Southerners! We're going to have to beat them. North versus South." Some of the players would protest, "Coach Hayes, the Civil War has already been fought and won." But he ignored the comments because he wanted to beat Alabama so badly.

Coach Hayes was clear in his expectations of his players. He adamantly forbade us from partaking in any of the debauchery readily available in New Orleans. He threatened the players that if he heard of any of us going to Bourton Street, he would call our parents to come and get us and we would not be playing in the game. Woody was trying to spare us the immoral sights and keep us focused on why we were in New Orleans – to win the Sugar Bowl.

I honestly think that arriving in New Orleans more than two weeks prior to the game was just too much time. Despite Hayes' warnings, there were many distractions, and being in a foreign city took us out of our normal routine. Whatever the reason, we suffered a scathing loss, 35-6, and flew home dejected. For me, this disappointment was motivation to focus more, work harder, and play smarter. I was still trying to make a name for myself, and I was more determined than ever to make a real contribution to this amazing football program.

I lettered my freshman year and ended up being a four-year letter winner. For those unfamiliar with the terminology, a letter is an actual letter monogram that is worn proudly on the jacket or sweater of the student participating in sports or other activities. It is earned after the player has demonstrated that he has something of value to contribute to the team.

My freshman football team was full of talent, and Coach Hayes was the most intense coach in my entire football career. He never missed an occasion to coach, ranging from coaching specific football plays to life coaching. Even the bus rides to practice were opportunities for us to run through timing drills in Hayes' eyes. Cadence drills were used to reinforce the physical synchronization necessary for effective play execution, and the mental discipline that led us to feel unified as a team. A cadence is used by a quarterback when calling plays to signal the timing of the ball snap to his teammates who would be familiar with the various cadences.

Coaches put the offense and defense players on separate buses to practice, and during the bus ride, the first team quarterback would stand up in the front of the bus to lead the drills. He would call a play and the cadence. The rest of us would then clap our hands together to imitate firing off the ball at the same time. If the rhythm was not in sequence, Coach Hayes would know that someone went offsides, meaning a player prematurely moved, and he would say, "You just cost us a penalty."

Coach Hayes was always thinking, always looking at how to make us better and how to keep our minds focused on what we were doing. His continual message was, "Stay away from the negative people who are going the wrong way, and surround yourself with people who are doing the right thing." This is a model I have followed my entire life, and one that I have always tried to instill in my own children.

Coach Woody Hayes was a teacher as well as a coach, and academic excellence was a high priority for him. He was always checking up on his players, encouraging us to take advantage of the special tutoring available, and discouraging us from hanging around with people on campus who exhibited apathy toward education. The word "apathy" came up in one of the Word Power classes which was mandated and taught by Coach Hayes. In these teachings, he often found ways to emphasize that there were a lot of lazy people on campus who were not doing anything productive with their lives, and that we should keep our distance from them. Avoiding bad influences was a recurring theme with Woody that, whether through repetition or resonance, sank in and affected how I make life choices.

Being away from home and family, I was missing the regular structure and fellowship of church. I still prayed, and there were others on the team that had religious backgrounds, but I needed more. Not long after arriving at Ohio State, I started a chapter of the Fellowship of Christian Athletes and invited some of the guys on the team to join. Being active in FCA taught me a lot about leadership, and this paid off for me, because by the time I became a senior, I was captain of the football team and voted Most Valuable Player. I matured dramatically during my freshman year, and it was almost hard to recognize myself when I thought back to the young man who walked into the dorm room only nine months earlier.

When the team returned to practices in late summer for the 1978 season, Vlade Janakievski, a great kicker for Ohio State, and Tyrone Hicks, the fastest guy on the team, roomed with me. Our room was right next to Coach Hayes' room, and we could hear the projector running late at night while he watched game films. One night just before the season opener, Coach Hayes wandered into our room while I was watching a football game on television. He sat down and watched the game with me, talking to me like a father to a son. He was very much a father figure to the players, and I felt especially to me.

Coach Hayes was definitely competitive, but to us players, it was obvious that we were his primary concern. He always thought about us first. He wanted to win games, no doubt about that, but he was most concerned about our well-being and in forging in us a noble character, sound life skills, and appreciation for knowledge. He made it clear that earning an astronomical salary was not his driving motivation when he responded to a journalist doing research for a documentary who commented, "You're one of the most successful college coaches in the country but yet you're one of the lowest paid." Coach Hayes responded, "If I would get more money,

I would be thinking more about my investments than I would be thinking about my boys." The parental care and guidance we felt extended beyond Woody to his wife, Anne, who remembered all of the players' names, knew our stories, where we came from, and made an effort to make us feel part of their family. It was a privilege to be included in this amazing family, and I openly welcomed it since mine was so far away.

Sometimes players (even me, on occasion) would start grumbling that practice was too hard or that muscles were hurting. Woody would, without a word, gather the complainers and load them on the bus to Children's Hospital. At the hospital, he would take us to visit with kids who had cancer, terminal illnesses, or were suffering with extreme burns. These children were so excited and happy to be meeting OSU football players, and we were moved by the huge smiles on their faces. The reasons for these visits were twofold. First, Coach Hayes wanted to show us why we should appreciate how trivial our complaints were, and second, he wanted to teach us to give back to our community. More than just telling, his coaching came in the form of teaching lessons with real life.

An essential component of The Ohio State University football experience is the marching band. Coach Hayes would arrange for the band to come to football practice and perform "Script Ohio" for the players, since we never got to watch the halftime show. Script Ohio, first performed in 1936, is an Ohio State University Marching Band tradition that remains an anticipated and entertaining halftime event. The 192 marching musicians file into a formation that spells out the word "Ohio" across the whole field, completed by a sousaphone player "dotting the i" to the robust cheers of thousands of loyal fans. Rarely, the university has selected an honorary "i-dotter" to recognize contributions to the university or Ohio. Coach Hayes was himself selected to "dot the i" in 1985. It just doesn't get any better than having The Best Damn Band in the Land give you a private performance!

My sophomore football season was very different from my freshman year. I hit my stride and saw a lot more game time, again earning a letter. In the third game of the season against Baylor University, I was in the right place at the right time when Ron Springs, the starting running back, got hurt. I was standing next to Coach Hayes and he turned to me, put the football in my arms and said, "Don't fumble. You're going in next." A wave of terror swept through my body. Nonetheless, I had fourteen rushes for a total of 97 yards. In the locker room after the game, Coach Hayes said to my dad, "He had a good game. The main thing is he didn't fumble!"

Overall, the season was a disappointing one for the team in that we didn't go to the Rose Bowl, but wound up going to the Gator Bowl, where we lost to Clemson. This game proved to be the end of Hayes' career at Ohio State, due to a momentary loss of control on his part during the game that led to him striking an opposing player.

I'll never forget when I heard the news. I was driving my parents back to Jersey from the Gator Bowl in Florida, and we heard the radio announcer say, "Ohio State has just fired Woody Hayes." I couldn't believe my ears. They didn't even bring the players back together and tell us. They only told the guys who were there locally in town. I was shocked and extremely saddened to lose my coach, mentor and friend so suddenly. Woody remained a teacher on campus despite being relieved of his coaching duties. I missed our daily interaction and hearing his stories. I would often visit him in his office, and enjoyed our talks very much.

When we got back to school, the Athletic Director told us that the new coach would be Earle Bruce. Most of us had never heard of him, but it turned out he was a former player and coach under Coach Hayes. Coach Bruce's coaching style differed from Woody's in many ways in that he concentrated on the business of the game and wasn't distracted by life lessons or intimate relationships with his team. I could talk to him, but not the same way I could talk to Coach Hayes. Coach Hayes was more the fatherly kind of figure, and Coach Bruce was more transactional. One thing Coach Bruce had in common with Coach Hayes was the importance they placed on academics. Coach Bruce had someone checking up on us and making sure we were going to class and that our grades were satisfactory.

By the time I was a junior, my coaches had determined that I had earned a full-time starting position. Coach Bruce's offense was different from Hayes', and I had to learn an entirely new way of playing. It was critical to me not to make mistakes, and I was determined to always be in the right place and doing my best job.

That year, at a home game against Washington State, I set a record for the longest touchdown pass reception (86 yards) in Buckeye history, that stood for 35 years. Just recently, my record was broken by a fine young athlete named Devin Smith during a game played at the University of California. His 90-yard TD pass reception replaced my record, but my kids still take pride in the fact that their dad still holds the record in the Horseshoe.

Due in large part to the coaching change at the end of the previous season, we were not ranked in the preseason polls, meaning we weren't assumed to be one of the top twenty-five teams. Previously, Ohio State had always been ranked in the top ten. Coach Hayes told us that even though he was no longer our coach, we needed to stick together. We took his advice, were unified as a team, and ended up undefeated and ranked number one in the nation.

One of our scheduled games early in the season was against UCLA at the Los Angeles Memorial Coliseum. Today, almost every college football game is televised, but it was a different time in 1979 with only a few college games getting national broadcast coverage. This game was aired on ABC, and I scored my first televised touchdown. The game was a tough battle but we never gave up, coming from behind in the last two minutes for a surprise win.

We were ecstatic with the win and could hardly contain ourselves as we started our journey back to Ohio. All of my teammates were singing the popular disco song "Ain't No Stoppin' Us Now" with customized lyrics of "Ain't no stoppin' us now, we're on our way to the Rose Bowl!" We knew we'd be visiting the state of California again that season. When we took off from Los Angeles, the pilot of the airplane that took us to Pasadena got permission to fly us over the Rose Bowl stadium. He tilted the plane to the left and to the right, so all the players could look down and see the Rose Bowl stadium. We looked down and yelled, "We'll be back!"

CHAPTER 4

THE ROSE BOWL

The Rose Bowl Game, considered The Granddaddy of Them All because it is the oldest bowl game and is the post-season showdown between the top-ranked teams from the Big Ten and the Pac-10 conferences. Things have changed over the years, and the Rose Bowl Game is no longer designated for these two teams but it was then, and continues to be, an honor to earn your place in Pasadena.

As we racked up wins through the season, our sights remained set on getting to the Rose Bowl. Our final regular season game was against Michigan, and we were predicted to win. We beat them 18-15 at their stadium in front of over 106,000 fans, the largest crowd ever assembled for a college football game. We were now the Big Ten champs and on our way to the 1980 Rose Bowl.

My dad came to every game, home and away, no matter where we were playing. My mom only came to the bowl games, because she was in New Jersey supporting my brothers who were still playing in high school. I fondly remember a game we were playing in Wisconsin. I was sitting out in the lobby chatting with some teammates before the game and in walked my dad. All the players came up, surrounded him, and said, "Okay, now we can play, 'cause Mr. Murray drove all the way from Jersey to come see us."

My dad was kind of the parent representative, because a lot of the guys' parents couldn't afford to attend the games. But when they saw my dad, it was an inspiration for them to work hard. They said, "Mr. Murray made the effort to support us, so we've got to do our best to win this game."

20

My parents didn't have a lot of money either, so my dad drove instead of flew to games, including the bowls. The exception was the 1980 Rose Bowl Game.

When my home town of Woodbine found out that I would be going to the Rose Bowl, they took up a generous collection and paid for my mom's and dad's flights, so they could make sure they were there to see me play. That's how important it was to the little town of Woodbine to have their town represented at such a momentous event, and to make sure my parents were there to see it.

Our Rose Bowl game was played on January 1, 1980 against number-three-ranked University of Southern California. The bowl game capped the end of a great season, and during the game, I caught a critical third-down pass that set up a field goal giving us a six-point lead. However, in the fourth quarter, I sustained a severe concussion and had to be removed from the game. We had many opportunities to win that game but lost by one point, 17-16. It was a gut-wrenching heart-breaker.

My senior year at OSU was in many ways disappointing. Although finishing with nine regular season wins, most of the wins were not the decisive wins they should have been. The team didn't play the way we should have and our ranking languished, eventually dropping to fifteen by the end of the season. We started with a number-one ranking, and we just didn't live up to the expectations. We lost our last game against Michigan at home, and we lost our last bowl game, the Fiesta Bowl. Going out my senior year on back-to-back losses was difficult and frustrating, standing in stark contrast to my junior year.

Despite our underwhelming performance, I earned two significant awards. I was voted the 1980 Team Captain of The Ohio State Buckeyes, and at the end of that senior year, the team voted me Most Valuable Player. It meant a lot to me that the players saw me as a strong leader. I called my MVP award my Heisman trophy. I was once told by someone I looked up to in high school that I wasn't cut out to be a leader or a captain.

This just showed me that when G-d put things on a bigger stage, I *did* have the qualities to be a leader.

CHAPTER 5

GOAL # 2 – PLAY FOOTBALL FOR THE PHILADELPHIA EAGLES

Could that really be? The NFL team I wanted to play for since 9th grade wants *me*? In the fourth round of the 1981 NFL football draft, the Philadelphia Eagles picked me! I later asked Coach Dick Vermeil, "Why did you draft me?" He answered, "Anybody who rushes for over one hundred yards against UCLA has to be a great running back." Coach Vermeil was a caring and honorable coach who really believed in me and taught me a lot of great principles. I always look forward to seeing him and catching up at NFL alumni events.

A lot happened between the end of my last football season with OSU and assuming my position with the Eagles. I left school to return to New Jersey, married, and was blessed with the first of two sons, Calvin Jr. I was so grateful to G-d to welcome this young man into our family, the first of the next generation. In the summer, I left New Jersey again to head to West Chester, Pennsylvania for the Eagles' training camp.

Shortly after arriving in Pennsylvania, a Philadelphia news station started a segment called "Diary of a Rookie" about my journey leaving south Jersey, going to Ohio State, coming back, and then being drafted by the Philadelphia Eagles. The news station reported on my progress every week, and as a young man, I certainly enjoyed being treated like a celebrity.

I played for the Philadelphia Eagles throughout the entire pre-season, but at the last roster reduction I was cut from the team as number fifty-one on a fifty-man roster. I went home to New Jersey and waited. And waited. I wasn't sure if or when I would get called back, so I kept working out to stay in playing shape. Other teams solicited me while I was waiting, but Coach Vermeil told me that he would bring me back at the first opportunity. I had wanted desperately to play for the Eagles since I was in pee-wee league, so I put off the other teams in the hopes I would hear from the Eagles. Coach kept his word, and five or six games later somebody got injured, opening a spot for me. I was really going to get to play an official, regular-season game in the green and white jersey!

The first game following my return, we were playing the Dallas Cowboys on their home field. This was a momentous occasion, because that was the first time I saw Tony Dorsett and other great Cowboys up close. I remember seeing the famous black hat of Tom Landry, the Cowboys' head coach. He was noted for his distinctive dress with a black suit jacket, and he always wore a black fedora. I admit I was a little star-struck.

Settling in with the team, I recognized I was again missing the structure of religious study in my life, and that some of the other players might be feeling the same. I suggested conducting a Bible study, and several teammates agreed. Over time word spread as far as the Philadelphia Phillies baseball team and the 76-ers basketball team, which meant I was leading assemblies of some well-known professional athletes at my apartment.

Prior to one of our sessions, I received a surprise call from Julius "Dr. J" Erving who was playing in the NBA for the Philadelphia 76ers. I assume he had heard about the Bible study from another player, but I don't know how he found my phone number. He wanted to let me know he and his wife were planning to come. He was probably the biggest celebrity guest we ever had, and it was quite a thrill for me to meet him.

I continued to play with the Eagles for the remainder of the 1981-82 season. After I got cut a second time, I bounced around for a few seasons. I played for the Arizona Wranglers, part of the now-defunct United States Football League, for the '83-'84 season. I was then traded to the Denver Gold for one season, and then back to the Philadelphia Eagles. After the third cut from Philly, someone from the San Diego Chargers contacted me. But before I could get to California, Philadelphia called me to come back again.

This time, I was even more determined to keep my spot on the team. I worked harder than ever. I was laser-focused! Then the player representative called me into the office and said, his eyes conveying his bewilderment, "I've never had to do this. You've done everything right to make this team. I don't know why we're doing this." They cut me again. This news really devastated me, because I had done everything they asked me to do and then some. I felt I outperformed other running backs; I put in more time, more effort than others; I prayed and didn't get into any trouble. And they cut me. This was the toughest test of my faith I had faced up to that point. It was hard to pick myself up from this.

Religion and my relationship with G-d were always central to my well-being and what I turned to when facing challenges. When I was playing for the Denver Gold, Head Coach Craig Morton paid me a compliment that I was later able to draw on for strength. We had a run of seven losses on the heels of seven straight wins, sending us into a deep rut of despair. I had continued my tradition of establishing a forum for like-minded teammates to discuss the place the Bible held in our lives as I moved through the teams in the USFL and NFL, and Coach Morton saw that Denver was no different. Rather than wallowing in the disappointment of the season, Coach said to me, "I've played with many great athletes, but you showed me what it means to be a Christian and an athlete because you put G-d first. You faced all kinds of adversity and never gave up. That's what made me recommit my life back to G-d. I want to thank you for what you've done for me." It was so gratifying to have made a difference in someone's life, and remembering this helped me put things into perspective after my recent change in career trajectory.

I ended up back in Columbus, Ohio, and ran into Mike Tomczak and Jim Lachey, former Buckeyes and current NFL players. During the off-season, they started a traveling basketball team called Ohio Buckeyes that played for charity. They asked me to join their team, and I was happy for the distraction. It was therapeutic to do something good for others, just like it was when Woody Hayes would take us to Children's Hospital. Tomczak, who was playing for the Chicago Bears at that time, was approached by a player personnel representative and asked, "Do you know of any running backs that we can bring in for camp? We need some guys to come in and help our players with training." Mike told him, "Yeah, I play basketball with Cal Murray. He's in shape. He can come in and get the job done." And just like that, I was brought on with the Chicago Bears a week before training camp started. These weren't just any Bears; they were the '85 Super Bowl Bears. I was awestruck and, after my recent defeats, acutely aware of my privilege.

As I had done so many times before, I assembled a group of players for a weekly Bible study almost as soon as I arrived at the Bears' training camp. The day of this first Bible study ended up being the last day of my football career.

We were conducting full team goal line practice, which means it's like a real-life game situation. The intensity was high as the coaches were making this an actual challenge between offense and defense. The quarterback called the play, which involved me carrying the ball. As I was running up through the middle, I got hit hard by several defensive players. As I lay on the field, I was overcome with terror, as I realized I was numb from the waist down. I started screaming, "I can't feel my legs!" Everyone standing on the field quickly realized it was serious, and made way for the emergency medical personnel who were rushing out on the field to examine me. I was taken off the field on a stretcher and loaded into the ambulance.

At the hospital, after the examination, the doctors told me that my career was over; I could not sustain another hit of any kind. The doctor said, "You have a narrow spine and can't play professional football anymore. The next time you get hit, there's a strong chance you could be paralyzed and never walk again." I can tell you, at that moment, my *brain* was paralyzed from the thought of my career being over just that fast. What a blow, right when things were looking positive. You learn in life that things can change in an instant. I was only 27 years old!

After the doctors told me my career was over, I tried to tell myself they were right, but I also was in denial, thinking somehow I could overcome my injury. Surely, G-d understands this is what I've been working for my whole life and will heal me so I can get back on the field. As time went by; however, I realized that G-d was the one who ended my career and was taking me down a different path. Finally, I realized that if I chose to continue playing football despite the warnings, I could very likely end up in a wheelchair. With a family to support, this was a gamble I was not willing to take.

When my football career ended, I was despondent for some time. Sometimes, even today, I succumb to thinking about why some of the guys who were doing drugs and behaving badly seemed to excel with their football careers, and mine was over so soon. It just didn't seem fair that I was trying to do the right thing, and the career that I loved and put my heart and soul into came to an abrupt and premature end. I learned a number of cliché lessons: life isn't always fair, appreciate what you have when you have it, and don't assume that it will last forever.

During this dark and troubling time, there was one ray of light that prompted me to call out to G-d to give me some clarity: my second son, Andrew Joseph, was born.

As my football career was ending, so was my marriage. I went to work at Health Power for a friend and mentor from my Ohio State days, Dr. Bernard Master. Over the years I had sought him out for advice on all topics, and this was a good time for me to be in regular contact with him. Unfortunately, it was too late to rebuild my marriage, and not long after settling in, we separated. I found myself in the role of a single dad to my two sons, Cal, Jr. and Andrew.

I wasn't in a great place, suffering the loss of my football career and my marriage. And at same time I lost my beloved father, who was only 50 years old. I was feeling extremely dejected, and was only able to get through this stressful period with G-d's help. I committed myself to my boys completely, and made no plans to remarry until they were grown. I was very involved with my church and stayed focused on making sure my sons had the right support, love and counseling they needed to get through this difficult time.

There was only one more goal from that list I made so many years back. I had played football for the Ohio State Buckeyes and the Philadelphia Eagles, so I could cross those off the list. I was very busy managing the mail room at Health Power, participating in various church activities and raising Cal, Jr. and Andrew, so that third goal was going to have to wait for now.

CHAPTER 6

JERI'S STORY

I was born September 1, 1958 in Newark, Ohio, fondly referred to as "Nerk" by the locals. September 1st of that year happened to fall on Labor Day, and that's exactly what it was for my mother. Newark lies 33 miles east of Columbus, Ohio, at the junction of the north and south forks of the Licking River. It is known for The Newark Earthworks built by the Hopewell Indians, and is a National Historic Landmark. These Earthworks are preserved in Mound Builders Park, a place I spent quite a bit of time in while I was growing up.

I was the first child of Nancy and Gerald (Jerry) Weaver, high school sweethearts who married shortly after graduation. They were living in an upstairs apartment of a building owned by my dad's parents. Eighteen years later, when I graduated from high school, I moved back into this same apartment to live on my own. While they lived there, it was tastefully decorated and prudently childproofed for my siblings and me, but when I took over, it was a different story. My grandpa indulged my every 1970s décor whim, even painting the walls with wild colors. It served them as a lovely home for a young family just as well as it served me for my own first digs.

My parents had a son, Carey, two and a half years after me and a daughter, Lori, four years later. In the early years, my mom was so busy cleaning, cooking and attending to three kids that I really don't have any memory of her sitting down to take a break. She was very committed to running a well-organized household where everything had its place and was put there when not in use, the kids were clean, and meals were prepared on time. She loved the nesting part of being a wife and mother and claims that was evident in early childhood by how she cared for her dolls.

Although she seemed to always be in motion, Mom did find time to do special things with and for us. She was a decent seamstress and would sometimes make our clothes, one time even making matching outfits for my best friend and me. Beyond that, she applied her sewing skills to making clothes for my Barbie dolls. I viewed them as "designer" outfits compared to what was found in the dime store. I felt loved that she handmade dresses and coats for my dolls.

My dad was an avid hunter and fisherman. He would regularly hunt and bring home squirrels and rabbits for dinner. The rest of my family would enjoy these types of food, but I never cared for them. One day, he came home from fishing with a big snapping turtle, which my grandma made into turtle soup. I was totally repulsed at the thought of eating a turtle! Maybe this was good training for the kosher diet I would later adopt.

My dad worked at Owens Corning Fiberglas as a machinist, a job he held until he retired at the age of sixty. For most of my upbringing, my mom was a homemaker. Later, when I was in mid-elementary school, she went to work as a secretary for the United Appeal. In her forties, still with three kids at home, she enrolled at Owens Technical College and earned her Nursing degree. While I didn't fully understand it at the time, I later came to appreciate her desire to make a difference in the medical world.

I marvel at my mother's dedication to pursue a degree and her passion so many years after graduating from high school. She enjoyed a rewarding career as an emergency room nurse, retiring after twenty years. I learned valuable lessons about perseverance and hard work from my mom, and I have been deeply inspired by her. Seeing her strength and tenacity taught me that, with the right mindset, I could do anything I wanted. Adopting those traits as my own has served me well in my life journey; in particular with my conversion to Judaism.

The house where I grew up was a short walking distance to my dad's parents, Grandma and Grandpa Weaver, and I easily spent as much time at their house as I did in my own. I was fortunate to have extended family living nearby as well: my cousin Kelly, an uncle, great aunts, a great uncle, and another set of grandparents.

I spent a great deal of time with Grandma Elsie Weaver and we developed a special relationship. We would ride the bus to downtown Newark to do banking, take care of business at the courthouse, and of course, to shop at the Woolworth and Kresge department stores. After shopping, we would sit on stools at the Woolworth lunch counter and order grilled cheese sandwiches, french fries and milkshakes. While such a simple activity, this is forever locked in my memory as a precious moment of time with my grandma.

Grandma was an excellent and prolific baker and cook, often hosting big family dinners at her house. She started my meal preparation training on the Easy Bake Oven she bought for my birthday, but quickly moved on to showing me how to shuck beans and can vegetables from the garden. She was still in her own kitchen making elaborate and nutritious meals at 92 years of age.

My mom was also a skilled cook, and prepared delicious meals for the family, but she preferred to do it herself while the kids were playing, so most of what I learned about cooking came from my grandma. That time with Grandma Weaver prepared me to feed the large family I was to have and to produce the extravagant Shabbat meals I would be cooking in the future.

Sometimes, we just played at Grandma's while she did her household chores. We played dress up with the old fashioned skirts, hats, jewelry, and satin gloves she stored in a large wooden trunk, we put on elegant tea parties with a little china tea set, and played outside in the sandbox or on the swing set. In the fall, Carey, Lori and I would rake the piles of leaves collected under the huge trees into "leaf houses," house-shaped formations sectioned into rooms. I loved the crackle and the smell of the leaves as we busily moved them from place to place.

Many summer days, I would get on my blue bicycle and ride up and down the roads, enjoying the wind in my face and the freedom I felt. Sometimes I would fill the basket on my bike with a few apples and ride down the dirt road to where a horse was kept. I would feed the horse an apple and continue on my bike ride, often stopping at a natural spring along the road to get a drink of the cold, fresh water. Yosef and I are zealous cyclists and often ride out into the country, which brings back these memories. I loved playing outside, and I think this is sadly missing in the lives of children today: not enough time in the fresh air and far too much time inside with faces buried in electronics.

My Grandpa Weaver owned a grocery store called Weaver's Market. He would give my friends and me little brown sacks to go behind the candy counter and load up. I felt proud that my grandpa owned a store, and especially one that bore my last name.

Mom's parents, Grandma and Grandpa Martin, lived only a few miles away from my home. My mom was the oldest of three with a sister, Barbara, two years her junior and brother, John, nine years younger. They are my only aunt and uncle, since my dad was an only child.

From a very early age, Uncle John was an avid collector of reptiles and arachnids. Much to my grandma's chagrin, he kept a wide variety of snakes, lizards, and turtles caged in his room. She was terrified of snakes, but indulged her son in his reptile interests, as long as he kept the bedroom door shut so she didn't have to see them.

One day when Grandma Martin was at the kitchen sink doing dishes, she had the intense feeling the she was being watched. The hair on the back of her neck bristled and, barely moving a muscle, she slowly pivoted her body to look behind her. There, slithering about on the tile floor were seven snakes!

She frantically called the switchboard at Denison University, where Grandpa Martin worked, and cried, "Tell Bill the snakes are out!" Assuming the worst, he immediately rushed home and ran into the house with a large snake hook, ready to wrangle the escapees back to their cages. When he rounded the door into the kitchen, he found seven overturned cereal bowls in the middle of the floor with saucers on top that Grandma had used to trap the snakes.

Turns out, it was not the large snakes that had escaped but just some crafty eastern hognose babies that found the ventilation holes in the cage lid. Remarkably, Grandma was able to gather her wits enough to contain them under the cereal bowls while she was waiting for Grandpa to come.

Newark, Ohio was an idyllic place to grow up, very typically small-town America. It was safe to walk or bicycle all over town, which I did on a daily basis. My childhood years were filled with Girl Scouts, dance lessons, slumber parties, school, sports, friends, and family activities.

My best friend for much of my elementary years lived across the street from me. We were opposites physically: she very tall and large-boned and I short and petite. We walked to Benjamin Franklin Elementary School together every day, and I had to take twice as many steps, twice as fast, to make up for the difference in our strides. To this day, I outpace most people with my speed-walking – maybe I owe it to her. Some of the nicknames ascribed to me growing up were, Squirt, Small-Fry, Shrimp, and Munchkin. Let's just say, I was rather petite.

In 5th grade, all students were administered a musical aptitude test on which I performed "off the charts" for violin. Excited at the news and wanting to foster their firstborn's hidden talent, my parents promptly enrolled me in lessons. When it was time to go to pick out an instrument from the music store, none was small enough for me to play so they had to have a specially-made, tiny violin. Despite the aptitude and parental support, I had no interest in playing the violin, and wasn't exactly cooperative with practice; thus, my stint as a violinist was short-lived.

One thing I did not have any trouble practicing was dance. At the age of four, I began spending many hours at Joan Garrett Dance Studio studying tap and jazz. I excelled in tap and was really able to shine. I still enjoy tap dancing and, over my adult years, have taken many tap classes to continue pursuing this interest.

Once a year, the dance studio put on a recital at the historic Midland Theatre in downtown Newark. I loved the beautiful costumes and intense rehearsals. What a thrill it was to perform to a packed house!

A second love of my childhood was reading, and this has endured into adulthood. I could not get enough books. I could usually be found sitting in the glider on the front porch or laying in the hammock in the backyard reading Highlights for Children magazines or Nancy Drew Mysteries books. If not at home, I was often at the library in downtown Newark. I would pick a book off the shelf and find a spot in the library to read. I was fortunate that this love for books and reading was nurtured by my family.

Another thing that seemed to be a spiritual attraction for me was the Christian book store located downtown. I used to like to go there and look at all the different kinds of Bibles, and when I had a little change in my pocket, I would buy a bookmark or trinket of some sort. There just seemed to be something comforting and meaningful about this place.

I participated in Girl Scouts, and fondly remember the weekly meetings at the leader's house, just one block away from where I lived. When it came time for the yearly Girl Scout cookie sale, I traipsed all over the south end of Newark peddling my wares. I was always working on a particular badge for my uniform, which my mom lovingly sewed onto my sash as soon as I earned each one. Our Girl Scout troop took trips, went to camp, made crafts, and learned manners, and how to be good and productive members of society. Going to Camp Wakatomika in Utica, Ohio for three weeks each summer was the highlight of the year.

My family never took big vacations to distant locations, but we did have two special places to enjoy family time together. The first was my Grandma and Grandpa Weaver's cabin, situated on twenty acres of dense woods about a 30-minute drive into the country. This primitive cabin, with no bathroom and a pump in the kitchen used to draw water, served as a hunting cabin and summer weekend retreat for the family. The one large room housed the dining table, living room and sleeping areas consisting of a set of triple-decker bunk beds on either side of the fireplace. My siblings and I would

34

sometimes start bickering about who would sleep on the very top before we even got there.

Outside, there was a large screened-in porch with a swing where I would snuggle in with my pillow, blanket and books, when not climbing the apple tree or playing on the swing set. My favorite activity was going down to the creek where we would swim, wade, catch tadpoles, and go fishing. The occasional snake stretched across the bridge would send us squealing, until Dad chased it away. Later, this locale would become a focal point of our family picnics, with our kids, nieces and nephews looking forward to braving the leap from the covered bridge to the creek below. Almost every year another young family member would face the rite of passage with shaky knees.

The second family vacation spot was the river cabin located on the Muskingum River in Zanesville, Ohio, about a 50-minute drive from our house in Newark. Because of its location on the river, we spent most of our time on the water fishing, skiing, and swimming at the sand bars. I liked fishing off the dock with my brother and dad, but the task of baiting the hook grossed me out. I would beg both of them to bait my hook for me, but my dad always refused, saying, "If you want to fish, you need to bait your own hook." My brother sometimes did it for me, but when he was feeling ornery, he would refuse. In those cases, to spare my bare fingers, I used gum wrappers to pick up the slimy worm and put it on the hook. Usually, the end result was my worm flying one way and my line the other. Dad would threaten to end my good time, complaining the bait was expensive, and if I wasn't going to do it correctly, I couldn't fish. Carey would more often than not give in and do it for me.

These were happy times, because we were all doing things we enjoyed, and we were doing them together. We spent so much time outside, communing with nature and with each other. Life seemingly just went along with minimal bumps. We kids were content and didn't want for much. My parents were present, involved and appeared to be jointly nurturing the young family.

The Christmas Season kicked off in Newark with the annual courthouse lighting on the Friday after Thanksgiving. Hundreds of people, including our family, would line the sidewalks with wide eyes, anticipating that magical moment when the Licking County Courthouse would come alive with bright and twinkling lights.

Most people would follow suit and decorate their homes for the holiday, and we were no exception. Rudolph and all the reindeer graced our roof from Thanksgiving to New Year's. During the Christmas holiday season my mom, dad, brother, sister and I often bundled up on a cold night and piled into the car to drive up and down streets all over Newark, looking at all the Christmas lights.

Holidays were celebrated only secularly, because none of my immediate or extended family was religious. I remember my parents and grandparents putting out small manger displays at the holidays, but nothing else of a religious nature was found in their houses, and never was there any conversation about G-d. Christmas was about Santa, the Christmas tree and presents; Easter was about coloring eggs and looking for Easter baskets.

Even though I had no religious instruction at home and we didn't attend church, it turned out that I was exposed to all types of worship, from Bible-thumping Pentecostal to Methodist, and from Catholic to non-denominational, through friends whose families did attend. On most Sundays, I tagged along with one friend or another to some sort of church. One particular year, my best friend and her family attended a Pentecostal church where pants and haircutting for women and girls were prohibited. It took some getting used to seeing them swim in their backyard pool in a dress or skirt.

The services at this church were lively and intense. I remember one time my mom picked me up from the church and could hear the loud singing and clapping emanating from the building. She had never experienced anything like this, and I think she was concerned I was going to become a holy roller! I chuckle at the thought that in a way, her concerns were realized, as I did become a committed Orthodox Jew, including modesty in dress and lots of lively singing during Friday night *Kabbalat Shabbat* services (mystical prelude to Shabbat).

Life changed dramatically for me when I was in the 7th grade. One day, out of the blue it seemed, my dad sat me on his knee and explained that he was moving out of our house. It felt like my world ended. Everything I knew to be true and dependable was uncertain. I had only ever heard my parents arguing once, and I did not see this coming. While I understand the reason my parents shielded us from their problems, it made it that much more difficult to comprehend when they decided to divorce. The divorce rocked my world.

We had barely adjusted to living separately from my dad when my mom remarried and moved us to the next town, Heath. For what surely seemed like good reasons to her, she waited to introduce us to this new man in her life until the wedding was imminent, but it resulted in having a virtual stranger for a stepdad. This marriage introduced a lot of turbulence into my life. I moved out of the house I had grown up in; I left my friends and extended family; I lost my daily interaction with Grandma Weaver; I tried to fit in at a new school. Combined with the usual difficulties fourteen-year-olds face, it was almost too much to bear. Obviously, I survived this experience, and I'm sure it was one experience that has made me stronger and more resilient.

I spent two-and-a-half years in this new house, and then my stepdad was transferred to Toledo, Ohio, a town nearly three hours away. Again, this was a devastating blow, in many ways. Although the move from Newark to Heath made it more difficult to spend time with Grandma Elsie, it was only a short drive, and I still saw her frequently. And, of course, I saw my dad regularly. This time, weekly visits with my dad and grandparents were not feasible. Visits were shorter and less frequent, which caused me to carry resentment toward my stepdad for moving us, and toward my parents for divorcing.

Despite the bitterness I felt about the move, I quickly settled into my new school, made new friends, and tried to carry on with the life of a teenager. But I missed my dad and, most of all, Grandma Weaver. I also missed my brother, who had stayed behind to live with my dad. During this time, I acquired two new sisters, Elisa and Erin, making me feel like I had a new family that was separate from my old one. Of course, there was a large age difference, fifteen years and seventeen years, respectively, and I was a busy high-schooler, so I was not too interested in these young additions to the family. However, we would become quite close as we got older.

One thing that kept me on track after we relocated to Toledo was being involved in an organization called Young Life. It was a non-denominational Christian ministry that reached out to adolescents in a non-judgmental way, to share G-d's love. I continued to have a thirst for spiritual fulfillment and a quest for religious truth. This group satisfied those needs for the time, and was what I needed during this stormy time. The two leaders of my particular group were keenly in tune with teenagers and their unique issues and challenges. I made new friends in this group, and my curiosity and love for the Bible quickly returned.

During the time I spent in Toledo, I not only attended school but worked at the local Bob Evans Restaurant, did some babysitting, hung out at the mall, and tried to adjust the best I could to a new place.

I was hired by Surface Combustion at the beginning of my senior year through the Cooperative Office Education program at my school. I worked there all school year, moving from one department to another as a floating secretary. The work was so enjoyable, I could imagine working for them for 30 years. After graduation, I was offered a permanent position. But by the end of summer, I was longing to return to my home town.

My dad drove to Toledo with a truck to pick up me and my belongings, and I left Toledo, never looking back. I moved right back into my grandparents' apartment where my parents had lived when I was born. Although my Grandpa Weaver was suffering from cancer, he worked tirelessly to repaint the little apartment in the colors I had chosen. My dad, brother, and grandparents were all thrilled that I had moved back to Newark, and would again be part of their lives on a regular basis.

At this point, I resumed my tap and jazz dance lessons, this time with a different dance studio. I was working full-time and was grateful to be back in my home town. However, within a few years, the "big city" of Columbus beckoned me. In Columbus, I continued to follow my passion for dance, auditioning to be a dancer for Vaud-Villities, a performing arts group. They selected me for a spring performance they put on every year at the Veterans' Memorial auditorium. This required several months of intense rehearsals, and costume fittings leading up to the big performance. I performed with them for two artistically fulfilling seasons.

While in Columbus, I got married and had two sons, Brandon and Corey. These two sons were the light of my life! Unfortunately, this marriage ended in divorce, and I found myself raising my sons as a single parent. It was a difficult time financially and otherwise. I knew that I could give my sons everything they needed, except one very important thing, and that was a positive male role model, a father figure. I contacted the Big Brothers/ Big Sisters organization, and was informed that there were hundreds of boys on the waiting list, and it could be years, if ever, that my sons would get a mentor. I then tried through my pastor to find a mentor, to no avail.

Every Sunday morning at church, I sat next to an elderly woman during services. She knew how disappointed I was that I could not find anyone from the church to mentor my sons. She told me one day after service that her daughter went to another church and there was a man there who was very involved with the youth, and she thought maybe he might be interested. Little did I know, this would be a turning point in my life and the lives of my sons. This is how I met my *bashert*, my soulmate.

CHAPTER 7

ANSWERED PRAYERS

Calvin was sitting in church one day and a woman came over and told him about a single parent from another church who was looking for a mentor for her two young boys. He told the woman he was interested, gave her his phone number, and asked her to have the boys' mother give him a call. A few months later, that long-ago conversation forgotten, Calvin's phone rang, and I said, "Hello, my name is Jeri. I'm the one who is interested in finding a big brother for my boys." From this moment, our lives were forever intertwined.

We thought it would be prudent to meet for the first time in a public place, so we met in the parking lot of Thomas Worthington High School where Calvin was a part-time football coach. After brief introductions, he opened the trunk of his car and took out two autographed footballs. This was a great way to break the ice with Brandon and Corey, who were a little guarded about meeting this stranger. As he expected, they were thrilled to receive such perfect gifts.

I think he had mentioned briefly his ties with football when we spoke, but I didn't realize he was actually someone famous until he gave these autographed footballs to my sons. Honestly, I was clueless about all things football. Much later in our relationship, Calvin commented, "I know you love me for me and not my notoriety, because you never heard of me." Very true – I just thought he was a nice guy who was going to be good for my kids. I knew at that first meeting that this mentor relationship was going to work, because I was immediately comfortable with him, and so were Brandon and Corey.

Calvin started taking Brandon and Corey to play putt-putt at the local golf range, to the park, and sometimes just to hang out at his house to play video games. He was so generous with his time and, knowing things were tight financially for me, he helped in so many ways. One night he took my sons out for dinner, and when he brought them back, they each had a new pair of shoes. It didn't take long to see that my boys were becoming attached to him. It also didn't take long for me to become attached to him! Calvin has said many times over the years, "You were looking for a big brother for your boys, but Hashem saw you needed a big daddy!"

Calvin and I were both raised in small towns by strong mothers and hard-working fathers, with extended family in close proximity, which, we quickly discovered, resulted in us having very similar life goals, values, and appreciation for family. Although my family life changed dramatically when my parents divorced and my mom remarried, the foundation of valuing a close family had been laid in the early years. We were surprised to find that in spite of the one glaring difference in our childhoods – religion being an integral part of Calvin's family and home life and it having no place in mine – we very much had the same commitment to our spirituality.

Within months of our first meeting, the six of us – Calvin and his two boys, my two boys and me – were sharing meals and spending leisure time together. An important point that anchored our relationship from the very beginning was our love of G-d and the Bible. Every night, after we put our kids to bed, we would read the Bible to each other on the phone, sometimes for hours. He was very involved in his church, and I in mine. We were both raising our kids in very similar ways: same values, same belief system, and similar types of churches.

When two adults with children start a relationship, it can be difficult to figure out when to introduce the kids to the new adults and to each other. And it can be difficult for the kids to accept new people into their lives. This was relatively smooth for us, given the nature of how we had started. My boys had their own relationship with Calvin before I did, and his boys had met mine before they had to think about being siblings. Calvin's Andrew and my Corey were both six years old, his Cal, Jr. was ten, and my Brandon was eight. Our own version of the Brady Bunch.

Our respective youngest sons, Andrew and Corey, were like two peas in a pod; their hearts instantly knit together. The two eldest, Cal, Jr. and Brandon, took slightly more time to warm up to one another. Of course, with both of them being first-borns, this was no surprise. But it did not take long; and before we knew it, they were the best of friends, too. It was amazing to see how well the four of them got along.

I was so impressed to see this man maintaining his own house, working two jobs to support his sons as best he could, and still finding time to volunteer with mine. I kept thinking to myself, "This guy is too good to be true!" He was kind. He was devout. He was honest. He was hard-working. So many wonderful qualities in one person.

In the course of our dating relationship, we took a trip to Woodbine, New Jersey, so Calvin could introduce us to his family. He wanted me to see where he grew up, and to meet his relatives. I met his brothers, sister, aunts, uncles, mother, and grandmothers. Sadly, his father had passed away the year before we met. Everyone welcomed us warmly, and his mother especially treated my two sons the same as she did her other grandchildren who were present. My boys felt the love in this home, as I did. In fact, I could picture us being a part of this wonderful, close-knit family.

Unbeknownst to me, Calvin had prayed a very specific prayer before we left. He prayed that if I were the right woman for him, the three women he respected most, his mother and two grandmothers, would let him know on their own accord. Of course, he did not communicate this with any of them prior to our trip. At separate moments during our visit, each of these women leaned in and told him, "She's the right one for you."

I had prayed for a role model for my boys, and I got the best one I could imagine. Calvin prayed for affirmation from the important women in his life that he had met the right woman for him, and they each came through. I wasn't looking for a partner, but here was this big-hearted, devoted man in my life, and he felt like an answer to a prayer I hadn't yet thought to pray.

CHAPTER 8

BLENDED FAMILIES

After a whirlwind romance, Calvin and I decided to bring our two families together in G-d's name, and build a life together. We knew this would present a unique set of challenges as we were merging our two families into one home. Brandon and Corey were moving out of their home and into a new one; Cal Jr. and Andrew were going to have to share their space with two new siblings; and all the kids were getting a new parental figure. Knowing marriages with step kids are more likely to end in divorce, and being absolutely committed to avoiding the nightmare of a second divorce for our kids, we took precautionary measures to avert or overcome the typical issues faced by families like ours. We read a book that gave us practical approaches to blended families, and took a class at Catholic Social Services for stepfamilies, which offered open discussion about common problems and solutions. We felt that equipping ourselves with coping strategies gave us a better chance of making our new family not only survive, but thrive.

We were married on June 20, 1992 in an intimate ceremony with only about 60 of our closest friends and family. Rather than the traditional giving away of the bride, we opted to walk down the aisle together with all four boys. We felt that it was important for them to feel included from the very beginning, and to understand that this was the making of a family, not just the joining of two individuals in marriage. I was particularly sensitive to this because of my experience with my parents' divorce and my mom's second marriage.

After the honeymoon, we settled into a routine of work, school, church, sports events, and running a household double the size to which we were accustomed. Calvin and I were working full-time, and the boys were in school as well as participating in a number of sports activities. Most days were carefully orchestrated affairs just to cover meals and transportation. Now that our children are adults and have more perspective on just what it takes to keep things moving, they look back on these times and wonder at how we did it. We know it was only with G-d's help.

Life became even more harried when we expanded our family with the blessing of our first son together, Isaiah Calvin, a year after our wedding. He was six weeks early, and was just a tiny speck of a thing. The other boys loved holding him so much that it got to the point Calvin and I practically had to make an appointment to have our turn. Isaiah was passed from one of us to the next continuously, only laying in his crib at night. We now had the makings of our own basketball team – five beautiful sons!

Fourteen months later, we were expecting our sixth child. When the day came for the ultrasound to find out the sex of the baby, our entire family was crowded around the table, eager to hear the announcement. When the doctor had the baby on the monitor, she said, "Well, I think you got it right this time. I think it's a girl!" Loud cheering and applause could be heard all over the doctor's office. The doctor said she should have ordered popcorn and snacks for the entire office. We couldn't have been happier with this news because we knew our family would not be quite complete without a daughter, and 22 weeks later, we were blessed to have Hannah Lynn join the family. If we thought Isaiah was spoiled by the older boys, we had no idea what spoiled was!

Each of our children is unique; and there are many stories to share from their childhoods. For now, I want to share one about each of them. Cal Jr., being the eldest, took his role very seriously. He told me that when he and his brothers were in elementary school, he would not let the bus driver leave the school until he did a headcount on each of his brothers every day. Once he had the headcount, Cal Jr. told the bus driver they could leave. He said he wasn't sure if his brothers ever knew about his "deal" with the bus driver! Also, there was a little store in our neighborhood by the name of Bear Hugs. It sold mostly small gifts, but they had candy as well. The four boys often would ride their bikes there to buy treats. Cal Jr. always had to be first. If any of the other boys would try to pass him, he would speed up, and make sure he was always first. "My motivation for Bear Hugs was that I was competitive; however, I also felt like I needed to guide my brothers and keep them safe. At the time, they thought I was always trying to win, which I kind of was; but I also felt obligated to lead them in the right direction. Especially because they were younger, and I didn't want anything to happen to them." They all looked up to him, and he was a good example for his younger brothers and sister.

Brandon, also being a first born, exhibited typical first-born traits: he was conscientious, an achiever, even something of a perfectionist. When Brandon was about seven years old, he decided to help me with some house cleaning. I had an antique and valuable cherry wood cabinet from my grandfather that had glass doors on the front. Brandon had previously helped me clean the glass. In an attempt to be helpful to me, he decided to clean not only the glass front, but the entire cabinet. With Windex, he proceeded to spray not only the glass, but all of the cherry wood, as well. Frightened when the wood turned white, sure that he had ruined the cabinet, he was crying his eyes out when I discovered him. Of course, I couldn't be mad at him for it; he didn't know any better, and was just trying to help me. Later on, I found some product at the hardware store that helped restore the wood. Brandon's traits of wanting to work hard to make things right helped him later in life, when he attended law school, and earned his Juris Doctor degree.

Now for Corey and Andrew, the two-peas-in-a-pod kids, a story from when they were ten years old. I have to preface this story by saying that we only disciplined our kids with spanking when they had committed a very serious infraction. We can no longer remember exactly what they did wrong. It may have been the time they punched holes in the wall of the inside of the garage. Calvin was so angry that they had done this that he told them to go to their room and he would be up shortly to spank them. He waited a few minutes, and when he opened the door to their room, there they stood with their football pads on! All I can assume is that they thought the pads would cushion the spanking. Anyway, they looked so cute and innocent, that all Calvin could do was laugh. He could not keep a straight face! Needless to say, the spanking never happened. He figured they were so scared thinking about it, if they had come up with the idea of the padding, that was enough torment for them.

From the time Isaiah was born, he had a love for nature, animals, and especially reptiles (much to my husband's consternation). When he was about five or six, he decided he wanted a pet snake. Given my childhood experiences with reptiles with Uncle John, I was comfortable with snakes or reptiles of any sort. My husband is terrified of snakes, but he did not want to discourage Isaiah from his passion. So, he devised a plan that he was sure offered no logical way Isaiah would be able to get a snake. He told Isaiah that if got the money to pay for the snake, the cage, the bedding, the light, and everything else he needed to set up the cage, he could get one. Where is a five-year-old going to get such money, right? Well, that was the end of that, or so my husband thought.

We were grocery shopping at Kroger's a short time later, and when we were loading the groceries in the van, Isaiah looked down and found a woman's purse. We took it home and looked through it to see if we could find identification. We found a driver's license, telephoned the woman, and soon she was at our door. She had been mugged in the parking lot at Kroger! She was so grateful for getting her purse back that she gave Isaiah a reward. Do you see where this story is going? The reward was enough for him to buy everything he needed to purchase the snake and the supplies! What was my husband to do? He knew he had to keep his vow to Isaiah, and so very soon, we had a baby ball python living with us! Isaiah loved this snake, and in fact the whole family did, except one.

Isaiah ended up having this snake for sixteen years. He would put it around his neck and carry it around the house and outside. I used to tell him that there wouldn't be a pizza place in town that would deliver to us because, when they knocked on the door, Isaiah would open it with this snake curled around his neck.

Hannah is and was from an early age very focused and very sure about what she wanted to be when she got older. She started telling us at about age seven that she wanted to be a nurse. My mother was a nurse and would always give Hannah her old stethoscopes and answer her questions about the field of nursing. Calvin and I would buy her doctor kits for her birthday. She was the one who would bandage cuts or treat bee stings. As of the writing of this book, she recently graduated from The Ohio State University School of Nursing, *magna cum laude*. She plans to continue her education and become a Certified Nurse Midwife. Like I said, focused, very focused!

On the weekends, we usually tried to do something fun and relaxing as a break from the frantic weekly schedule. We camped, bowled, rode rides at amusement parks, miniature golfed, and sometimes, just took the kids to the park to let them run off energy. The activities didn't matter, it was just important for us to have time to decompress as a family. Stories from some of these weekends still come up on the now too infrequent gatherings around the dinner table.

As busy as things were for us, we were still able to fit in the occasional extended trip. We visited the Boardwalk and beach in Jersey and vacationed in Myrtle Beach twice. By far, our favorite place was in Ohio, at Salt Fork State Park. We stayed in the 148-room lodge that offered indoor and outdoor pools, hot tub, air hockey and ping-pong tables, video games, shuffleboard, hiking trails and a lake with a beach. It had something for everyone, and no one ever complained of boredom.

At Salt Fork, our kids usually could be found in one of two places – in the pool or in the game room. The four older boys loved to challenge Dad to a game of ping-pong. However, as hard as they tried, they could never beat him! We have many, many fond memories of Salt Fork, some of which are preserved in treasured videos and photos. Every year, our very last activity on Sunday morning before we left was to capture the group in a family picture. Of course, all the kids were sad that it was time to leave, and the annual pictures show their forced smiles. Starting as soon as they woke up and continuing until we were in the car on the way back to Columbus, they would beg, "Can't we stay for just a little longer?" Looking back on those photos, it makes us realize how much these family getaways to this most special place meant to our children and to us. More important than the imperfect family photos were the memories we generated.

Church involvement was also a family affair. The boys loved Sunday school, Vacation Bible School, and church camp, and seemed to thrive in those settings. At the request of camp staff, Calvin began donning a costume and mask to play Mr. Amazing, a super-hero type Bible character. None of our boys knew at first that it was actually their dad who was running up and down the halls of the fellowship building, cape trailing behind. Eventually their suspicions started to take root when they realized Mr. Amazing would appear when Dad disappeared. In fun, they would try to grab his wig off to prove it was really Dad. Mr. Amazing occasionally showed up at church on Sunday mornings. Calvin and I also taught Sunday school, Vacation Bible School, and fulfilled other leadership roles in the church.

Our lives were filled with many sports activities, dominated by football, with all four older boys playing at various levels, and Isaiah catching football fever as soon as he was old enough to play. Some of the kids played soccer, some played floor hockey, some were on the jump rope team, and some played basketball and participated in track. Hannah was also an athlete, playing basketball, soccer and running track. Of course, this meant years and years of transporting them to practice, buying uniforms, sports pictures, doctor/ER visits for injuries, paying admission to games, gas money to get back and forth to out-of-town events, providing team meals, sports meetings, filling out paperwork, and on and on. The sports portion of our lives by itself was enough to fill every day. The amount of food I had to prepare to feed all these athletes is unimaginable. I cooked dinner every night, and not fifteen minutes later, the boys would be rummaging through the cupboards looking for a snack, telling me they were hungry again. It was an incredibly busy time in our lives and, looking back on it now, I don't know how we did it all without collapsing from exhaustion. Now that our kids are adults, they realize the sacrifices we made for them.

After we had child number six, we realized we needed to look for a larger house. Our family now numbered eight, and we were in a fairly small three-bedroom house. One day after church we were driving through Sharon Woods, a neighborhood that we really liked, and we saw a "For Sale" sign in front of a house that appealed to us. The owner was gracious enough to show us the house, and from the moment we walked inside, we felt that this was our new home. The house was huge, with six bedrooms, three bathrooms, an enormous master suite, and a fenced yard with a deck – everything our large family needed.

We were so excited and wanted to buy it right away. Sometimes Hashem says, "Yes," and sometimes, "No," and sometimes, "Not now." "Not now" was the answer we received, although it sounded a lot like "No" at the time. We made an offer on the house, but it was contingent, because someone else had beaten us to the punch and had the primary offer. Unfortunately, the primary offer went through and someone else bought the house. We were extremely disappointed, but realized that G-d is in charge, and for some reason we were not supposed to live there, at least not yet.

About two years later, when we were the youth pastors at a church close to this very house, we found out the house was back on the market. We quickly drove over and walked through again, just to make sure we still felt like it was to be our next home. We quickly made an offer, which was accepted. We just could not contain our excitement! Our current house sold quickly, and soon the big moving day arrived. That summer was spent packing, decluttering, and getting ready to move our family of eight to our new home. We moved in August, I think the hottest day that summer, definitely in the nineties and very humid. We lived in this house for fourteen years, until we had to sell it and move to the Jewish community.

The four older boys went to school outside the home, but Calvin and I decided that homeschooling the younger two was a good option. So began our eight-year homeschooling odyssey. These homeschooling days were some of my favorites. I loved being home with the kids, and they were involved in several formal homeschooling groups where they went once a week for gym, drama, creative writing, music, art, and other subjects. My friend Jill was homeschooling her three kids, and she and I would regularly take all the kids on interesting field trips. My mother would occasionally come from Toledo to teach the kids painting. I homeschooled them from kindergarten through part of middle school, and found creating the foundation of their education gratifying.

Blending our families was replete with bumps and turbulence along the way, but Calvin and I were committed to making it work, and work it has for the past 26 years. All families have their difficulties, and ours was no exception. We weathered these storms with teamwork, prayer, patience, forgiveness, and a lot of love. Most people who initially met us had no idea that we were a blended family. They thought the kids were ours together, and admired the love and cohesiveness they observed in our family.

CHAPTER 9

THE AHA! MOMENT

"Do you know the origins of Christmas?"

Of course we do. Don't we? As Christians, we put out our manger displays, exchange gifts, and attend church services to rejoice in the birth of Jesus. Surely, these conventions are based on the biblical story. Right? Calvin and I were going through the motions of religious observance as they had been taught, without ever considering why.

Our friend, who attended a church that embraced a somewhat more literal interpretation of the New Testament, asked us this seemingly innocuous question with the intention of provoking a thoughtful reflection of what the Bible says about honoring the birth of Christ. Knowing Calvin and I shared her innate desire for religious truth, she expected us to be surprised by what we learned and potentially to be dissuaded from continuing in what she felt was an inauthentic tradition. Her expectations were realized when Calvin and I found ourselves compelled to research the truth about why we celebrated the all-important Christian holiday the way we did.

We spent many hours at the library plowing through everything we could find on the subject. The most basic things were so starkly obvious: Jesus never commanded his followers to celebrate his birthday, and no mention of Christmas ever appears in the Christian Bible. In fact, many of the pagan observances were adopted by the Christian church as a means to attract more converts to Christianity.

We discovered this dearly-held holiday actually was very pagan at its core. These revelations absolutely shook our world – and these doubts were the beginnings of what came to be an undulating rumble, lasting many years.

After we recovered from the initial shock of our discovery, we took the first step to remove these distortions. We opted to trade the usual commercial trappings of Christmas – Santa, stockings, a tree, and gifts – for something more personal: we would go away for a family retreat. We settled on Salt Fork for all it had to offer, and visited for ten Christmases.

The kids took the cold-turkey cancellation of Christmas as they knew it in stride, and fully embraced the new Salt Fork tradition. It likely helped ease the transition that we gave each of them a set sum of money to spend as they wished. It also helped that Calvin and Andrew retained a traditional Christmas with their mother, as did Brandon and Corey, to a lesser degree, with their dad. Isaiah and Hannah were too young to realize the significance of the change. They all loved Salt Fork so much that, if given the choice, I'm confident they would have chosen to go to Salt Fork rather than have Christmas at home.

For Calvin and me, shedding the inevitable stress of the season and lingering credit card bills was a welcome relief. We felt we were better able to savor the time together and with our children and bond with them, rather than feeling frazzled and tense.

However, not everyone was supportive of this move. Some of our close family and friends felt we were depriving our children or setting them up for ridicule by doing something different than other families. Of course, they weren't deprived, because the older four still had a Christmas with their other parents, and we were confident they would get more out of the family trip than they ever would from a Christmas at home. Calvin and I were committed to our decision, feeling it was fundamentally the right thing to do. We did our best to ignore the naysayers, and were happily validated at the end of our first trip when the kids were begging to stay.

The visits to Salt Fork Lodge petered out once the older boys began graduating high school and moving on to college. In December 2016, we had a reunion there with all of our kids and grandkids. It was wonderfully surreal to see several of our kids with their kids in the same pool and running around the same lodge as they did when they were younger.

When Calvin and I married and merged our families, we agreed to find a new church for all of us rather than pick his or mine. After a great deal of visiting, we settled on one that met our needs. However, it wasn't long before we were back at my church, because we wanted our kids to attend the school with which it was affiliated, and it made sense to also rejoin the church as well. As at previous churches, Calvin and I were involved with the youth, and participated in Bible studies and events in addition to the Sunday services. A few years in, Calvin was wanting to more formally work with youth, and there were no positions available at our church, so we began hunting again.

At the same time, someone who knew of our involvement with youth told us about a church in the north suburbs of Columbus that was looking for a new youth pastor. We decided to check out this church to see if it was a place we would fit in and feel comfortable. We spent time meeting families and getting involved, and right away, we felt like this was a place we could call our spiritual home. My husband applied for consideration and was hired. As with most youth pastor positions, a husband and wife team is preferred, so I too became involved. We delivered a weekly sermon, taught a mid-week Bible class, and provided counseling and spiritual guidance to the junior and senior high youth. We had a number of administrative duties that included scheduling and supervising field trips, recruiting teens for a yearly conference, as well as fundraising, designing curricula, administering the Sunday school program, and preparing a budget.

Our kids settled into this new church nicely and, needless to say, the youth were drawn to my husband like a magnet. They knew he cared deeply for them. This position was a labor-intensive second job for us, but we were wholly committed, and enjoyed the overwhelming connection to the church and its congregation. Although we continued to examine the questions we had about Christianity, we still viewed ourselves as staunch Christians, and experienced several happy years as members of this church.

Still, my friend's simple question about the pagan origins of Christmas reawakened in me the quest for truth that had been my spiritual motivation since youth. Once we began to question and study, the dam began to crumble, pushing us to question more and more of the Christian doctrines we had held near and dear. I believe that Hashem saw our sincere desire to follow Him at all costs, and over the next several years, He gave us the strength to persevere in our truth-seeking.

Although to a degree happy and fulfilled with our church and spirituality, we could not ignore the nagging struggle we had with what we were learning. If Jesus was a Jew, and Christians are to follow the example of Christ, why aren't we observing Jewish laws? If Jesus would have celebrated Shabbat, why is our church service on Sunday? If Jesus would not have eaten pork, why are we having a pig roast at the church? We weren't asking why we weren't Jews, just why these Jewish laws weren't also part of our observance. No one at our church could answer this to our satisfaction, and we sensed our questions were raising concerns about our faith among our congregation.

Christianity is not exactly a faith system that encourages critical thinking or questioning; it is based on accepting the doctrine on belief and faith, with little discussion of evidence. While all religions include the faith tenet in one way or another, as we were later exposed to other groups of Christians who were willing to discuss these topics, we realized that we could be dutiful to G-d, and still ask questions.

Having lived through our journey from being Christians to living as Orthodox Jews, it feels as if it was just taking one sensible step after another. Very logical. Very progressive. Very gradual. To outsiders, and maybe some insiders, our journey from Christianity to Judaism seems a drastic and abrupt change in beliefs. It is difficult, even impossible, to understand how this happened without evaluating the incremental movements and the catalyst for opening our minds to exploration.

We didn't recognize it at the time, but that benign question – "Do you know the origins of Christmas?" – was the catalyst, the pivot point, in our spiritual life. If not for that question, we might never have asked other questions that redirected our trajectory toward Judaism. That was the beginning. That was the first event that caused us to start probing the purpose and origins of our beliefs and practices. It was the first time we considered why we were observing the way we were observing.

CHAPTER 10

THE MESSIANIC BRIDGE

Although we continued to ask questions and were learning things that poked holes in Christian theology, we still viewed ourselves as Christians, with an unwavering belief in Jesus as the messiah. We were not willing, or even able, to discard all we had been taught just because we couldn't quite make facts fit. But it did propel us to keep digging. We could not deny the nagging urge to learn more, with a desire to reconcile what we knew and believed about Christianity and the Bible. At this point, we were pursuing authentic Christianity, not Judaism.

We were very happy at the Christian church we were attending, and had built strong relationships with the kids in our youth program and their parents. For a couple of years, we attended services and ran the youth program while doing our religious study on our own time, because we did not feel encouraged to practice this line of questioning in the open with our fellow church leaders. Although studying on our own was somewhat haphazard at times, with no one to point us in a direction, it was vital that we uncover the truths in our own way and in our own time to allow our acceptance to happen naturally. Had any person, religious sect, or leader led us to conclusions, we would likely have been skeptical of agendas and unable to make the leap.

However, we were getting to a point where it was difficult to know where to look next. We were unsure of what else to study. We'd been through the Bible many times and still had unanswered questions. Then, a friend suggested we seek guidance from an organization that recognized, studied, and observed the Jewish roots of the Christian religion, thus opening our eyes to the messianic movement.

This congregation has some Jewish elements, but is thoroughly Christian in its mission, believing that Torah observance is exclusive to Jews. In addition to holding their services on Saturday, you will see *kippahs* (yarmulkes, or skullcaps) and *talleisim* (garments with ritual fringes) being worn, Hebrew classes in session, and the Jewish holidays celebrated in some measure, but always with a Christian spin.

Until we were asked about the origins of Christmas, we had never given any real consideration to the fact that the roots of Christianity are Jewish. Although we were taught that Jesus was a Jew, how this fits with the rest of the Christian story was never explored in our churches. The experience in the messianic congregation was really our first exposure to Judaism of any sort, and we felt emboldened to explore these questions with the leaders and members.

We began attending the Saturday service, took a few classes on the Sabbath and Jewish holidays, and I began taking a Hebrew class one evening a week at the messianic congregation, all while maintaining our prominent positions in the Christian church. The more we discovered, the more intrigued we became, and the deeper we wanted to delve. We were positively captivated by what we were learning, and felt increasingly drawn to Judaism, even at this early stage.

We were brimming with excitement over what we were learning at the messianic church and eager to share some of this beauty with our youth group. Church leaders staunchly opposed our efforts. They told us, "We're not a Jewish synagogue and we don't want any of that Jewish stuff in here." Understandably, they were concerned that we were rejecting Jesus, although that thought had never crossed our minds at that point, and we assured them this was not the case. The leader of the messianic congregation even called the pastor of our church on our behalf to reassure him that we were not questioning this most important tenet of Christianity.

We had no objective other than to share what we were learning. It wasn't about teaching Judaism to our students or contradicting anything they knew and believed about Christianity. For us, it was about enhancing what they knew and striving toward authenticity. In hindsight, it was a legitimate concern of our church leaders, as maybe they saw something happening with us that we had not yet acknowledged.

During this time, we heard about another messianic organization that holds an annual conference for learning. The conference spans three days, including Shabbat, around *Shavuos* (holiday commemorating the giving of the Torah on Mt. Sinai, celebrated seven weeks after Passover). Several hundred people travel from around the globe to attend the workshops, commune with like-minded believers, and strengthen their faith through education. We attended that year in Arizona out of sheer curiosity, thinking it would be, at a minimum, a nice getaway for the two of us.

The focus of that first conference was that Torah observance was not only for Jews, but for Gentiles as well. This was quite a shock, since it contradicted the position of our local messianic community. The conference leaders' argument for Gentile observance was especially convincing because they based it directly on Christian scriptures. Deep in our souls, this felt right. More pieces of the puzzle were falling into place.

The conference hosted a Shabbat dinner outside in the courtyard of the hotel, and it was truly a beautiful introduction to a sacred institution of the Jewish Sabbath. Trees and flowers surrounded the courtyard where the tables were set with gorgeous dinner service, and a violinist was walking around softly playing music. The intoxicating ambiance and connection with other attendees made the event a memorable highlight for Calvin and me.

We felt so fulfilled by the teachings, interactions, and experiences at the conference that we quickly decided we would return the following year. In fact, we returned for eight years to places like Phoenix, Houston, Pennsylvania, and Wisconsin, each occasion filled with many learning opportunities, Shabbat dinners, reconnecting with old friends, and meeting new ones.

Most of the families that attended these conferences were homeschooling families whose values and beliefs were consistent with ours. Every year we added to our extended truth-seeking family. At the first conference in Phoenix, we invited a woman to join us for breakfast one morning. It turned out Sarah was from very near us in Ohio, living less than an hour away from our home. Sarah was the first of so many new friends we found through the conference association, and she became very important to us. She traveled with us to all subsequent conferences, and I even joined her on an Israel trip a few years later.

At later conferences, three more families were introduced to and became enthusiastic participants in our journey: the Bittings, the Sharrocks and the Southwells. The Sharrocks were from Ohio, the Bittings from Texas, and the Southwells travelled all the way from Australia to take advantage of conference offerings. The Weeks family, also from Ohio, had become a part of our Shabbat home group and they attended the conferences as well. These truth-seeking families, deeply committed to their children and to their relationship with G-d. Our relationships with them, individually and collectively, strengthened our fortitude for pursuing spiritual growth.

One person in particular from the families we met was April. We discovered right away that our love of homeschooling created a strong bond between us. But our connection went much deeper. I felt like my soul and April's were somehow knitted together. April, too, would travel with me to Israel for an archaeological study tour, and visited when Calvin and I were there in 2014.

It was a wonderful environment in which to take part. Of the four families with whom we became close, three of us have completed halachic conversions to Judaism.

The conference in the Poconos (Pennsylvania) proved to be a pivotal point in our learning, because it introduced us to the discipline of fixed-time prayers. The title of the conference was "Pray in the Spirit," and it focused on the thrice-daily Jewish prayers. The purpose was to challenge us to incorporate traditional Jewish liturgy into our communities and private prayer lives. This was our first real introduction to *davening* (Jewish prayer), and we were just overwhelmed with the beauty and meaning in Shacharis, Mincha and Maariv, There were several workshops explaining the origins and meaning behind these prayers. We accepted the challenge by incorporating some of these prayers in our regular routine.

Every year, there were several hundred people, beautiful families, in-depth teaching, guest speakers, kosher food, and lots of fun. It was the only time during the year we felt at home, surrounded by several hundred like-minded people, slowly increasing our knowledge about Judaism.

At what turned out to be the last of the conferences we attended, in 2007, the focus was answering anti-missionary arguments. Anti-missionary activists work to combat the proselytization and recruitment of Jews by Christian religious groups. The emphasis of this conference was a response to those efforts and the trend among many messianic Gentiles who were falling in love with Judaism and leaving Christianity altogether. They discussed an anti-missionary expert, Rabbi Tovia Singer, of whom we had no knowledge, and other anti-missionaries, who pointed out the errors and inconsistencies in the Christian scriptures. We heard, described in the most uncomplimentary terms, of some people who had left the faith and were now pursuing conversion to Judaism. We were strongly warned to stay away from these influences and not to associate with any "apostates" who had defected to Judaism. Although this message did not seem significant because it wasn't relevant to us, we thought we had better heed the warnings so as not to fall for any such teaching. We had no way of knowing that Rabbi Singer would appear in our future in a very substantial way.

These conferences afforded us wonderful opportunities to learn more about Judaism and to make friends with people who had outlooks similar to ours. Over our eight years of attendance, we increased our knowledge of Judaism, gaining a basic understanding of *Birkat Hamazon* (Grace after Meals), davening, the Torah service with *aliyot* (plural of aliyah, going up/the honor of being called up to read from the Torah), Jewish holidays, ritual hand washing, and many other Jewish practices. Even though we learned later that some of the content was erroneous, it gave us enough of an understanding of the Jewish roots of the Christian faith to allow us to begin thinking outside the box of Christianity, and to question certain tenets of the Christian faith.

When we visited the Beis Din for the first time, and shared with them our intention to convert and how we came to that decision, they commented that it makes perfect sense that many people who seek conversion come from the messianic movement, because that is where they are initially exposed to and learn about Judaism. Without being involved with the messianic movement, coming to Judaism would have probably come much later, if at all. The Jewish roots of the Christian faith were just not talked about in church. All throughout these conferences, Jesus was still worshipped and considered to be one and the same as G-d.

Attending these conferences year after year had the effect of chipping away at our faith system bit by bit, and we became increasingly disillusioned with the church and Christianity. They, in turn, were becoming increasingly concerned about us. It became uncomfortable to go to church on Sundays, and to listen to incorrect messages. Ultimately, the leadership of the church was concerned that we would teach these perceived fallacies of messianism to the youth, and Calvin was forced to resign.

The fallout of resigning the youth pastor position and leaving the church was painful. We realized severing our connection to the church effectively severed all the relationships we had built over the years. We ceased to hear from those we had called our friends who were part of that community. We suspect that church leaders warned people to stay away from us, that we were heretics who had willingly given up our salvation. Given our large youth group and parents who had been in regular contact with us, we expected some outreach. But, no one called to see how we were doing – not any of the pastors, not any of the congregants. Not one phone call. The silence was deafening.

This event caused us to take a hard look at the path ahead of us. The salary Calvin made as a youth pastor paid the mortgage. I was homeschooling the two youngest kids, and only worked occasionally. This was to be a huge test of faith. How would we meet our financial obligations? We were very committed to homeschooling, and for me to work full-time was the last option on the list. Honestly, looking back, it's hard to remember how we managed to make ends meet.

And, more importantly, we were a family without a spiritual community, essentially on an island, with no desire to go back and no idea how to go forward. We faced much soul-searching, and mustered an incredible amount of emunah and *bitachon* (trust) that G-d would somehow provide for our financial and religious needs. Ultimately, we prayed for Him to show us a clear and obvious path.

CHAPTER 11

RECALIBRATING

Within a few months of Calvin losing his job as youth pastor, my Grandma Weaver broke her hip. She was 92 years old and my dad had already passed, so she needed someone to care for her. I would not entertain the suggestion of putting her into a nursing home. My selfless and wonderful husband agreed that we would offer to take care of her in our home, to which Grandma agreed with one condition: that we accept $1,000 a month in payment for her care. She would not consider any other arrangement. Wow, talk about answered prayers! This monthly payment was just about the same salary Calvin was making in the part-time youth pastor position. It was "clear and obvious" to us that G-d quickly replaced the income stream we lost with Calvin's termination.

My grandmother could not manage stairs, so we converted our main floor dining room to be a bedroom for her. Since this room was right off the kitchen, a hub for our family, it allowed her to interact with family members and visitors throughout the day. I know this is part of what kept her happy and healthy for the next eight years, until she died just a few months shy of her 100th birthday.

Although we were steadfast in our decision and happy to do it, taking care of Grandma was a tremendous responsibility and sacrifice for my husband, my kids, and me. It also was a tremendous blessing. Everyone pitched in to assist her and make sure she wasn't left alone. I believe that there are valuable lessons about being selfless, caring for elders, and dedication to family that my children learned in taking care of her. It was a symbiotic arrangement; we gave her the kind of care only a family can give, and she gave us life lessons and companionship only she could give us.

With the financial concern addressed, it was time to make a decision about our options for spiritual nourishment – either we could find a new church or join the messianic congregation officially. Neither one felt exactly right.

We were at a point in our development, after attending the yearly out-of-state messianic conferences, that the local messianic congregation was no longer a good fit. The teachers at the yearly conferences taught that Jesus was a Torah-observant Jew, and given this, the Torah was also for Gentiles; therefore, we should be observing some measure of Shabbat, *kashrus* (Jewish dietary law), and so on. The local messianic congregation believed the opposite – no Torah for Gentiles. As we learned more, we preferred the approach taught at the conferences, and ended our association with the local messianic chapter.

Without another apparent option, Calvin and I decided to form our own group with two other couples. Our fledging group met every Shabbat for most of the day, enjoying study, prayer and a potluck. We studied the Christian Bible (New Testament), but also utilized the Chumash and various Jewish commentaries. We celebrated the Jewish holidays the best we knew how: fasting on Yom Kippur, hosting Purim and Hanukkah parties, and conducting *Pesach Seders,* (Feast that includes reading, drinking wine, telling stories, eating special foods and singing, commemorating the anniversary of our nation's miraculous exodus from Egyptian slavery more than 3,000 years ago) but always with a Christian spin.

We advertised our group on several messianic websites so like-minded people could find us. Quickly, our group grew to include as many as 40 people on Shabbat from across the state of Ohio. Henry and Judith, one of the founding couples, lived on a large piece of property, and would always host our group for the yearly Sukkot celebration, complete with a bonfire and camping overnight. This fellowship and group study made us realize we definitely identified with the Jewish people and Israel.

By this time, Hannah and Isaiah were approaching high school age, and Calvin and I decided to end home schooling. We were in a dilemma about where to send them based on their individual needs, our religious standards, and our financial means. We quickly ruled out the public school, based on academic deficiencies, and we had reservations about the Catholic school the four older boys attended. While Bishop Watterson offered excellent academics, the religion classes and required Mass attendance were at odds with our beliefs. Isaiah wanted to play football, and Watterson offered a solid football program. To add to the deliberation, Isaiah would receive a tuition grant at Watterson, which would alleviate the financial strain on the family. In the end, we decided he would follow in the older four boys' footsteps.

Choosing a school for Hannah presented a second debate. We wanted a school where she would be challenged scholastically and receive religious nurturing that was not contrary to what she was finding at home. Given our current spiritual trajectory, we initially looked into a local Jewish school, Columbus Torah Academy. We met with headmaster Rabbi Zvi Kahn to tour the school and to evaluate the educational offerings. Right away, we were struck with his warmth and openness to a non-Jewish prospective student and family.

After the tour, Rabbi Kahn asked us why we would consider his school for our daughter. We told him of the route we had taken from Christianity to the messianic movement to Judaism home study in as much detail as time allowed. He said, "Wait a minute. You mean you are on a search for truth, and when you find it, you just pursue it regardless of the consequences?"

We responded, "Yes, that's pretty much it."

After a brief pause, he "You have to come to my house and tell my wife and kids your story. It's so inspiring!"

Rabbi Kahn reined in his excitement about us after we agreed to meet his family so we could discuss Hannah's interest in the school. He was concerned that she had not studied any Hebrew, and indicated that this would be a major hurdle. The other students received Hebrew instruction from a young age, and Hannah would be at a disadvantage. He concluded the meeting by agreeing to meet with his colleagues to determine whether Hannah would be accepted as a student.

We soon received the disappointing news from Rabbi Kahn that he and the administration had decided not to accept Hannah. They felt she would be frustrated and discouraged by her lack of Hebrew knowledge while also trying to fit in with the Jewish students. We couldn't argue with their assessment and agreed it was for the best.

Although we were hoping for a different outcome, we were happy to discover an unexpected, wonderful friendship with the Kahns. Meeting Rabbi and Mrs. Sara Beth Kahn and their wonderful children opened a new inlet to the Jewish community, and they offered us much encouragement and advice along the way.

After visiting other schools, Hannah ended up selecting Tree of Life, a Christian school, where she excelled. Everything turned out just as it should have. Although it was an unexpected turn of events, we consider meeting the Kahns to be one of the clear and obvious signs we were looking for on our spiritual journey. We are so very thankful to Hashem for bringing our lives together.

During the homeschooling days, when Isaiah and Hannah were working on assignments, I would frequently listen to the online Israeli radio station, *Arutz Sheva* (Channel 7, known in English as Israel National News), and happened upon a program hosted by Rabbi Jeremy Gimpel and Rabbi Tovia Singer. The program format consisted of people calling in to ask the rabbis questions about Judaism, Christianity, and Israel.

Rabbi Singer. Where had I heard that name before? Ah, yes, he was the very same Rabbi Singer the messianic conference leaders warned us to avoid for his anti-missionary stance. Rabbi Singer is the director of Outreach Judaism, an organization dedicated to countering the efforts of Christian groups who specifically target Jews for conversion. We were told he was dangerous to our faith.

But I was captivated and could not stop listening. The things he said resonated deeply with me because they made so much sense. He answered some of my long-standing questions, but his answers generated even more questions.

As a Hebrew language authority, he pointed out the mistranslations of the Hebrew contained in the Christian Bible, how things were taken out of context, and how they were even changed to fit Christian ideology. I immediately ordered his *Let's Get Biblical* book, and began intensely studying it. One of the things that impressed me about Rabbi Singer was his extensive knowledge of the New Testament. It was clear that he understood the New Testament better than most Christians did, even better than many pastors. He is widely regarded as one of the world's leading experts on Christian evangelism.

Of course, I could not wait to share the information and the radio programs I had listened to with Calvin. I expected him to be as intrigued and excited about the new information as I was. He was not. He reacted strongly, telling me he was not interested in hearing anything about this. He was staunchly resistant to even considering the idea that what he had always been taught could be wrong. I understood this was a turning point for him, and thought that with time, he would get back in step with me and want to know more.

In an effort to break down his personal wall around the Bible, I would periodically ask Calvin a question about a mistranslation in the New Testament. He would instantly become defensive and tell me that if I questioned anything about Jesus or the Christian faith, he was not going to travel that road with me. Contrary to my hope, time was not motivating him to resume the pursuit of truth with me. In fact, he was frankly telling me I would be traveling the rest of this trek alone.

Looking back, I think Calvin was unable to take the next step because of the deep devotion to Jesus that was ingrained in his upbringing. A singular Christian belief system was the thread used to weave his family life, church life, and school life from the time he was born. Challenging the accuracy of the Bible so directly would feel like taking scissors to that fabric and destroying it snip by snip. It was too much to consider.

I was likely more open to what I was reading about the manipulation of the Bible because I didn't have one religious system that I lived by my entire life. Instead, I had always had an instinctive quest for spirituality and truth that drove me to keep looking for the right fit. When I was a kid, I would attend different churches with my friends, appreciating what I observed, without necessarily being compelled to get more involved. During my young adult years, I found Christianity to be a good fit and committed wholly to the beliefs, but there were always questions. Ever since we had discovered the true origins of Christmas, I felt the magnetic pull to the place I knew would be the perfect fit. I didn't know where that was, but I felt this path was the way there.

I felt myself being drawn to Judaism, yet still desperately trying to hold onto Jesus. And, of course, wanting to keep peace in my marriage. But even my belief in Jesus was starting to slip away. The more I studied the Tanakh regarding the role and purpose of the messiah, the more I realized it could not possibly be the Jesus I revered. A strong feeling of uneasiness was setting in. Without Jesus as the foundation of the Christian faith, the rest of the pillars of Christianity begin to fall away.

I had always grappled with the two sections of the Bible, the Old Testament (Jewish) and the New Testament (Christian). I was taught that the New Testament was a continuation of the Old Testament, which never made any sense to me, because the two books are so obviously dissimilar. I couldn't get past the following question: If Jesus died for the sins of all mankind, and professing belief in and allegiance to him was the only way to go to Heaven, what about the people mentioned in the so-called Old Testament, such as Moses, Abraham, King David, and Joseph? Obviously, they never heard of Jesus, so are they burning in hell? I was frequently told that these Old Testament people somehow knew about Jesus, which seemed illogical to me.

I continued to hide Rabbi Singer's book under my side of the bed, and did not let Calvin know what I was studying. About this time, I became aware of another anti-missionary organization called Jews for Judaism, and of Rabbi Michael Skobac. This organization helps keep Jews Jewish, and gives them tools to refute the Christian missionaries. I listened to many online lectures given by Rabbi Skobac to further my understanding and validate what I was finding in other sources.

I did not want to be on a divergent path from Calvin. I wanted him to discover the truth *with* me, so I continued to broach the topic from time to time. Every once in a while, I would throw out a question about an inconsistency in the Bible, to which he would reply, "I'm not going there." I was patient and, grudgingly, he finally agreed to listen to some of the recordings and study some of the materials I had been studying. He says he was finally able to get past his resistance because he knew we had great trust and communication in our marriage, and he was willing to make a concession in light of my unyielding determination to pursue this line of questioning. I think he drew a line between the process (studying) and the potential conclusion (conversion) in order to take this step. By agreeing to review the material with me, he was committing to look at it, but not to accept it.

We made a special time during the week to dig in and take an honest look at our beliefs. We would spread all our materials around our dining room table and comb through the Christian Bible, Rabbi Singer's book, and other commentaries, to evaluate contradictions and confirmations. There came a moment after months of intense studying when even Calvin could not deny what we were learning, and we were forced to admit that Christianity had seriously tampered with the Jewish scriptures.

Each week, Calvin and I would pick a particular belief about Christianity that had already perplexed us or had become increasingly problematic, to either validate or invalidate, as the case may be. One such belief is the doctrine of the trinity, that G-d is present in three entities – the Father, Son and the Holy Spirit. This is opposed to the Jewish understanding that G-d is one, and not a man. Of course, there is no mention in the Torah of a trinitarian G-d. Many other issues began to surface as well, such as the immaculate conception, the virgin birth, Jesus' resurrection after being crucified, and Jesus being crucified to atone for the sins of mankind – concepts that were held dear and precious in the Christian Bible. Calvin could not deny what he was seeing with his own eyes, and became propelled along the path with the same force I was. We were back in lockstep.

Perhaps the most troubling, and, in the end, the most compelling contradiction that we found impossible to reconcile, was that of the status of messiah assigned to Jesus. The messianic prophecies contained in the Jewish Scriptures state that the messiah will bring world peace, establish a universal knowledge of G-d, facilitate the gathering of the exiles back to Israel, build the Third Temple, and more. The Christian messiah clearly did not fulfill or accomplish any of these prophecies. Of course, the church's response to this colossal problem is a second coming, that Jesus will accomplish these things when he comes again. There is no concept of the messiah coming, failing in his mission, and coming again in the Tanakh. But this is Christianity's rationalization of Jesus' failure to function in any way as a messiah or fulfill any of the prophecies in the Tanakh.

We gradually began to see that Christianity had used a tool to suit its purposes called "Biblical revisionism," where a deliberate alteration of the original Hebrew is used to prove a point. Other machinations became obvious as well, such as verses taken completely out of context, mistranslation of the original Hebrew, adding words, changing the meaning of words, or even inventing a verse that does not exist.

The religious foundation we had grown up with, raised our children with, built our home on, crumbled. The spiritual house, so to speak, tumbled down. Where do we go from here? Ignore what we have learned and choose not to rock the boat with our kids and family? Go back to the church or messianic congregation and sit as skeptics?

Or, do we change religions? Changing religions would turn our family's world upside down; but we had to consider this as an option. There was no other place to go.

Even though we diverged for part of this journey to Judaism, once Calvin started studying, he soon realized where we were headed, and that what he was studying was *emes*. He patiently listened to my concerns and questions, and then researched for himself. We grew together step-by-step in Judaism and in marriage. I'm so very thankful that we were on this journey together. I'm grateful that there were no arguments or hard feelings. He had to find it himself, but we were together in this. It was **our** decision to leave the church, to convert.

CHAPTER 12

THE BIBLE: LIVE

In early 2007, through a series of events that can only be described as Divine Providence, I had the privilege of visiting Israel for the first time. My friend Sarah, the one we met at the first messianic conference in Phoenix, had planned to return to Israel for her eighth time on an archaeological study tour. After her traveling companion had to cancel, Sarah asked me if I wanted to go. I did. Desperately. The thought of seeing with my own eyes the places I had read about in the Bible and walking in the Holy Land was like a dream.

But there were so many obstacles. Grandma Weaver required someone to be home and, even though Calvin and the kids helped with this responsibility, I didn't feel I could ask them to cover it completely while I left for two weeks. With two kids in private schools and two others in college, we did not have the money sitting around for a trip like this. So, I initially told Sarah I didn't see how it could work. In the meantime, Sarah had been told that it wasn't as simple as substituting me for her friend that had cancelled. The trip organizers maintained a waitlist and would have to add me to the bottom, making it very unlikely that I would secure a spot anyway.

I resigned myself to not being able to join this trip and went on about life. One day I received a call from the trip organizers telling me that I had a spot on the tour if I wanted it. The open spot had to be filled by a woman in order to room with Sarah, and it turned out the people above me on the waitlist were men. This raised a whole new excitement. I probably wouldn't have pursued it any further, but my generous and selfless husband told me he wanted me to have this experience, and he would take care of all the responsibilities at home. It was hard to accept his offer, because I knew it would be a hardship for the family. But I was also inexplicably drawn to Israel, and I couldn't resist the urge to start figuring out how to clear the money hurdle.

Calvin was working full-time, I was working part-time at a law firm, and we had the stipend from Grandma, but there just wasn't any discretionary income, given our expenses. I had talked with a friend from the law firm where I was working about this opportunity and that I was trying to figure out how I could possibly pay for it. She suggested I have a yard sale and ask people to donate items. I thought there was no way I'd make enough money from a yard sale to cover the cost, but maybe it would be a start. Every little bit would help me get closer to the goal. Never one to back away from a challenge, I started making plans for the sale. I put word out to people I knew from work, with neighbors, friends, and family. Before I knew it our garage was filled to overflowing with clothes, exercise equipment, household goods, and small furniture.

I arranged to hold the sale on a Friday and Sunday, allowing for our Saturday Shabbat observance. My mom insisted I needed to include Saturday in the sale if we wanted to make any money, but I was adamant in my decision. I was sure if G-d wanted this to happen for me, He would provide, while allowing for the Sabbath.

That Friday morning, we spread out all the goods, covering the driveway, yard, and garage. It was a very hot, sunny day and people came out, first in a trickle and then in droves. I had advertised in local papers, hoping to get the traffic necessary to sell all the items we had collected. My primary goal was, of course, to make money to contribute to my Israel trip, but I also didn't want to have to deal with a bunch of unsold belongings. By the end of the day, I had collected over $1,200! Sunday was rainy and we had less traffic, as expected, but still raised an additional $300.

Two families we had befriended at the messianic conferences, the Sharrocks and the Southwells, each sent me $300 out of the goodness of their hearts. This, combined with the proceeds of my yard sale, provided the funds necessary for the trip. I never expected to raise as much money as I did with the sale and, certainly, didn't expect donations from friends; but this proved to me I was meant to go to Israel. I was meant to experience live the locations of the stories I had read.

The name of the tour was "Walking the Ancient Paths," described as a study of the land which would include scaling mountain slopes, sloshing through Hezekiah's tunnel and other underground water systems, sailing on the *Kinneret* (Sea of Galilee), and shopping in the Old City of Jerusalem, as well as Ben Yehuda Street, and the famous Mahane Yehuda Market (fondly known as "the Shuk"). It was a physically demanding tour, requiring participants to be able to endure long hikes, climb and descend multiple sets of steep and sometimes uneven stairs, and clamber along treacherous slopes.

Not merely for tourists interested in shopping or seeing the most famous sites, this tour was intended for people interested in experiencing the land from the vantage point of the Biblical text. Detailed maps and a field book were provided several months prior to the trip. Each day consisted of eight to twelve hours of treks to several Biblical sites with on-bus lectures, and optional lectures in the evenings. It was an exhausting trip with full days of touring, walking, praying and studying. Much emphasis was placed on trade routes used during Biblical times. We got to map, travel and walk these same routes. The tour was led by two brothers, one a professional historical geographer, specializing in the land of Israel, and the other a leader of a messianic congregation.

One day involved a harrowing hike down a steep cliff on Mount Arbel at Arbel National Park and Nature Reserve in the Lower Galilee region. The Arbel Cliffs offer breathtaking and majestic views overlooking the Sea of Galilee, the Golan Heights, and Mt. Hermon. Our guides divided the group into two camps – one that would go back to the bus and wait (for reasons of health, or simply because they did not relish mountain climbing), and the second that would venture down the mountainside. Wisely, Sarah chose to wait on the bus. I thought, "How bad could it be? I'm physically fit and adventurous!" I thought it would be a moderate walk down a rock-strewn path.

I seriously underestimated the precariousness of the descent. Rather than a face-forward walk down, it was a backward climb down the face of the mountain, with metal hand and toeholds driven into the rock. I struggled greatly to reach the toeholds with my kid-sized legs, and wearing a skirt only made it more difficult. I realized part of the way down that I was hanging off the side of a mountain, and that one wrong move would have me fall forty feet or more. I managed to survive this experience with G-d's help. When I arrived back at the bus, Sarah was smiling, very glad that she was in the "smart" group.

Before visiting Israel, of course, you read the Bible and likely believe it, but when you are actually standing on those stones, seeing those places live, it strengthens your emunah. Israel was a place that had seemed so far away, both physically and spiritually, from where I was. But now, it was no longer about words on a page – the reality of walking the land overwhelmed me.

I had some sense of what a trip to Israel would be like, but nothing could have prepared me for the intense spirituality of walking the Land. I just kept saying over and over again, "I'm in Israel!" It was very surreal. Up to that point, Israel was just a place I read about, but actually being there was profoundly life-changing. This trip developed my love of the people, the land, and the Scriptures.

At the end of each day, our legs were tired, but our hearts were charged with a deeper appreciation for the Biblical world. There were forty-two of us in the group who started out as strangers, but we quickly formed a bond that in many cases was to last for years.

I was so affected by my experiences in the Holy Land that that when I returned, I gushed and gushed about the trip to just about anyone who would listen. April, having played a role in getting me to Israel in the first place, had been there herself a couple of times. I couldn't wait to go back, and kept telling her how great it would be to go together. In 2008, April and I took an almost identical trip as my first.

The itinerary was virtually the same as the previous year's. Even the lodging and the activities were the same. It made no difference to me that it was a repeat; I went with the attitude that I could always learn something more. April and I grew closer during this trip, as you often do with companions while in a foreign land. We appreciated studying together and physically exerting ourselves every day.

One of our favorite places was Nof Ginosar Kibbutz, located on the shores of the Kinneret. We stayed for a couple of days and nights on the lush grounds, where hammocks and swings swayed in the breeze. It was a very serene and peaceful place. We ate fresh and delicious dates that had fallen off the tree, and dipped our feet into the water at the private beach, while reading the weekly Torah portion. It was a special place where we could focus on Hashem and revel in His creation.

The first time you go to Israel, you are a bit overwhelmed with the culture and language, and just getting your bearings in a strange place. During this second trip, things became a bit clearer. I was able to figure out where I was in the country, and I was more able to take in all aspects of the experience, because I wasn't so overwhelmed. I knew what to expect; places and concepts were more familiar, and I felt more at home.

PHOTOS

CALVIN MURRAY | THE OHIO STATE UNIVERSITY VS. UNIVERSITY OF MICHIGAN | 1979

CALVIN MURRAY | PHILADELPHIA EAGLES VS. ST. LOUIS CARDINALS | 1981

EMUNAH'S MATERNAL GRANDPARENTS
ROSAMOND & WILLIAM

EMUNAH'S FATHER, JERRY

EMUNAH'S BROTHER, CAREY EMUNAH'S PATERNAL GRANDMOTHER, ELSIE

ANNUAL MOTHER DAUGHTER TRIP | ERIN, LORI, JERI, MOM, ELISA | 2012

YOSEF'S SIBLINGS, YOSEF, GLEN, YOSEF'S MOTHER, CAROL, DONNA, JEFFREY & JERRY

YOSEF'S PATERNAL GRANDMOTHER, OPHELIA

YOSEF'S PARENTS
CAROL & LEON

YOSEF'S MATERNAL GRANDMOTHER, ANNABELLE

WEDDING | JUNE 1992

SALT FORK | 2001

FAMILY REUNION AT SALT FORK | 2016

CAL JR'S WEDDING | 2008

SALT FORK | 2016

SUCCOS IN ISRAEL | 2013

EMUNAH AND HANNAH'S
VOLUNTEER TRIP TO ISRAEL | 2011

ISRAEL | 2017

KIDDUSH AFTER THE MIKVAH | 2013 | EMUNAH'S MOTHER, NANCY, APRIL, YERACHMIEL, YOSEF & EMUNAH

KIDDUSH AT THE CONVERSION: RABBIS ACKERMAN, NEUSTADT, BERGSTEIN & SILBERBERG

MOM, EMUNAH & HANNAH AT THE CONVERSION

CHUPPAH | MARCH 3, 2013

REBBETZIN ACKERMAN WALKING EMUNAH TO CHUPPAH

RABBI AREYAH KALTMANN SIGNING THE KETUBAH

ESCORTED TO YICHUD BY RABBI CHAIM ACKERMAN

YOSEF ON CAL JR'S SHOULDERS AT CHUPPAH

YOSEF AT CHUPPAH RECEPTION

JACK & SHELLEY, YOSEF & EMUNAH, PAUL & KATHY, DAVID & CATHY, DAVID & ANA

AVI, ADIRA, SARA BETH, ZVI, RENA & SHMUEL KAHN

RABBI CHAIM & CHANI CAPLAND

RABBI LEVI & AVIVA ANDRUSIER

RABBI AREYAH & ESTHER KALTMANN

RABBI YAKOV & JUDY GOLDBERG

EMUNAH & FRIEND RENA

EMUNAH & FRIEND, CHAYA BLUMA
IN BAT AYIN, YOM KIPPUR, 2017

DR. RIVKAH LAMBERT ADLER & RABBI ELAN ADLER

NETANYA FRIENDS: ANDEE, BARRY, WARREN, NADIA, SUE & ADELE

RUTI & AVI, YOSEF & EMUNAH | MA'ALE ADUMIM

EMUNAH WITH FRIEND, AHUVAH GRAY

CHAPTER 13

THE MEZUZAH IN MY PAST AND FUTURE

While our religious journey was progressing, things were changing in our household. We worshiped on Saturdays rather than Sundays, our family meals no longer contained any pork, I stopped wearing pants, Calvin was covering his head on Shabbat and wearing tzitzit tucked in, and I was covering my hair partially. We had dipped our toe into Jewish living, adding new elements with each conference we attended.

These changes were obvious to Hannah and Isaiah, who were still living at home and had attended the messianic conferences with us. The older kids, who visited often, also noticed the changes and would sometimes ask, "Are you guys turning Jewish?" For a long time the answer was, "No, we're learning more about what the original Hebrew Bible says and trying to live that way." But, eventually, as our direction changed, we did talk with them about our realizations.

Our extended family members were a little slower to catch on because, of course, they were living in other towns, and religion wasn't a regular topic of discussion with most of them. My mom and siblings thought of me as the religious zealot in the family, and likely viewed anything they noticed as just another shade of "being religious." No one questioned me directly about why we weren't answering calls on Saturdays or why I was dressing even more conservatively than I had in the past. They all knew I was deeply religious, and none of this raised any serious concerns with them.

Being several states away, we saw Calvin's family even less frequently, so there were relatively few opportunities for them to notice these subtle and not-so-subtle variations in our worship, and in our dietary and dress habits. Regardless, you might expect Calvin's family, whose values are steeped in

Christianity, to have a more contentious response to any perceived deviation from their religion that refusing meals containing pork and forgoing Sunday church attendance might evoke. Surprisingly, no one asked him pointedly about his interest in Judaism or accused him of betraying his faith. Some family members took to ribbing him by referring to him as "Calvin, the Jew," but none were seriously offended by the new observances.

On one of my mother's trips to Columbus to give Hannah and Isaiah an art lesson, she and I were standing in my kitchen chatting when she noticed a decorative Seder plate hanging on the wall. She casually mentioned that her mother firmly believed that her father was Jewish. I'm not even sure how she recognized the plate as Jewish; but it led to an enlightening and fascinating revelation.

My mother's mother, Rose, traveled to Los Angeles, California, in 1963 to visit her other daughter, Barbara. While there, she and my aunt attended a synagogue in the Valley on Friday nights. What prompted them to go there in the first place remains a mystery, but once she went, my aunt claims she couldn't tear her mother away. A one-week visit turned into three months, requiring my grandfather to mail her medicine, and ended with my aunt's decision to move back to Ohio.

I was stunned to hear this story for a couple of reasons. The fact that my grandmother took this trip at all is incredible because she was very much a homebody, dependent on my grandfather for most things, never even learning to drive. I had also never known her to have any religious affiliation or interest. I wondered why she had never spoken about it or pursued her curiosity about Judaism after returning from her California trip.

Mom went on to say, "John [my mom's brother] has some sort of Jewish pendant that Mom gave to him." She didn't know what it was or what it represented, but when she described it, I recognized it instantly as a *mezuzah* (a decorative case containing a Hebrew prayer, commonly hung on door posts). No one is sure when or where my grandmother purchased it, or even why, but she had it engraved and gave it to Uncle John when he was about sixteen.

Later, I contacted my uncle to find out more about the pendant and whether he still had it. He didn't know much about the origin or intention behind the gift, or even what it was, but had kept it all these years. He sent me a picture of it, and lo and behold, it was a sterling silver mezuzah pendant on which Grandma had engraved "To John, Love Mom." Preparing for a move to Australia from his longtime home in Arizona, John graciously passed what I consider to be a family heirloom on to me.

Mom went on to share during this conversation that her mother had written a letter to her children in 1985, about a year before her death. In this letter, she expressed a compelling need to share what she believed about her father's, my great-grandfather's, Jewish heritage.

I have known from early childhood that I heard from some source… that my father was not born to the Dashers. As I vividly recall my father's features, especially his eyes and mouth, I have known without a doubt for the past sixteen years that my father (your grandfather) was a Jew. Either the Dashers adopted him as a baby or he was given to them by the parents or by an unwed mother. So I do not know what his real name was; as neither Jack, Fred nor I know our true name. My father was known as John Edward Dasher.

…your children and grandchildren are richly blessed with Jewish beauty.

Signed "Love, Mom" she added a post script of advice to each of her children:

P.S. Nancy, glory in your Jewish heritage. Barbara, glory in your Jewish heritage. John, glory in your Jewish heritage.

What was thought to be an inexplicable attraction to the teachings at the California synagogue and affinity for the Jewish people was more likely a connection to her heritage. I could not believe the story my mom was relating to me. There was no way to prove what my grandmother had claimed, and *halachically* (according to Jewish law) she would not be Jewish because it was her father and not her mother; but still I feel it could explain some of my longing to connect to the Jewish people. These two family artifacts, the letter and mezuzah, represent to me my destiny as determined by Hashem, manifesting years later with fulfillment of the mitzvah of hanging of the mezuzahs in my Jewish home.

CHAPTER 14

"REAL" SHABBOS

After Calvin and I had come to terms with the realization that Jesus could not be the messiah, along with all the other Christian falsifications uncovered in our kitchen table sessions, the question of "Where do we go now?" resurfaced.

Somewhere along the way we had developed a distaste that was becoming stronger for the messianic movement as a whole. While the people we met in our congregation were pleasant and instrumental in advancing our understanding of the Bible, we had come to view the movement as misguided in its purpose. Aside from that, we couldn't very well continue attending the messianic congregation if we no longer subscribed to the ideology that Jesus is the way to salvation.

Our home-based group was chugging along, but turnout was inconsistent, sometimes only six of us convening for our potluck and Bible study. Many of the participants were traveling long distances to attend and had found other options closer to their homes. We enjoyed the fellowship of the group and felt it provided us the freedom to observe Jewish customs that were beyond what the messianic congregation was providing, but Calvin and I needed more.

We were not ready to say or even think the word "conversion" yet, but the brink was near. We needed to figure out where to go next for more organized observance and education. I was curious, and felt we would both benefit from attending a true Shabbos morning service in lieu of the Christianized version we'd been attending at the messianic congregation. I wanted to find a synagogue close to our home that demonstrated an openness to non-Jews, so the internet scouring commenced.

It didn't take long to discover the Lori Schottenstein Chabad Center (Chabad Columbus), just seven miles from our home. I sent them an email explaining we were not Jewish but very much wanted to experience an authentic synagogue service. Satisfying my concern about openness, Rebbetzin (Rabbi's wife) Esther Kaltmann responded to say we were most welcome to attend. I didn't comprehend at the time how monumental this invitation was for us, but it propelled us through what could have been a quagmire of doubt and uncertainty.

That very next Saturday, Calvin and I nervously walked into a synagogue for the first time. It was daunting to walk into this new place, not knowing a soul, to attend such a sacrosanct ceremony. But it was so exciting, too. We very much wanted to witness how "real" Jews "do Shabbos." We had been getting a Christianized version through the messianic congregation, and had been fumbling our way through our self-led Shabbos observance with the group, none of which felt exactly right. We wanted – no, needed – to see with our own eyes, hear with our own ears, and feel with our own hearts the "realness" of Judaism. Prior to the Shacharis service on Shabbos morning, Rebbetzin Kaltmann taught a women's *parasha* (section of the Torah read in the synagogue each week) class. A dozen or so women crowded around a table, attentively listening to Esther expound on the week's parasha. One particular woman in the class, Cindy, introduced herself after class and invited me to sit with her during service. Because of her kindness, I felt welcome and more at ease with the unfamiliarity of the service. She became a cheerleader for us later as we began the conversion process.

Despite being outsiders, we felt a sense of belonging, a connection to G-d, and a spirituality that was more genuinely satisfying than our Christian or messianic associations. There was a sense of familiarity because some service elements mirrored what we had experienced with the messianic services, but much was foreign. We were self-conscious for not knowing what to do, when to do it, or where we were supposed to be in the prayer book. We followed along as best we could, soaking up every bit of the experience.

Rabbi Areyeh Kaltmann, using humor and enthusiasm to connect with the congregants, expounded on what was read during each *aliyah* (the act of going up to read from the Torah) and explained the parasha. This Shabbos Shacharis service was an eye-opening experience for us and fully exceeded our expectations. We were awestruck. And we couldn't wait to come back.

Chabad, an acronym for *Chochmah* (wisdom), *Binah* (understanding) and *Da'at* (knowledge), is one of the largest and best known Hasidic movements in the world. Influenced by the teaching of the Baal Shem Tov, an 18th century Jew, it teaches the principal of finding the divine spark in each person and revealing it with unconditional love. Chabad Columbus conducts a number of outreach and education programs to unaffiliated Jews or Jews who are not very knowledgeable about Torah, *halacha* (Jewish law), and Jewish identity. There is no judgment, but only acceptance of where people are. Chabad Columbus assumes a Judaism 101 approach to those seeking to learn. Rabbi Kaltmann embodies the Chabad principles, and is adept at explaining not only what makes up Jewish practice, but *why* Jews do certain things, making this the perfect place for Calvin and me to take up our Jewish education.

It was spiritually nourishing and refreshing to be able to ask questions, any questions, without shame or fear of reprisals. The norm in Judaism is to dare to question and discuss everything. Here we found an outlet for intellectual questions and spiritual yearnings. Questioning is naturally inherent to the Jewish religion, which stresses learning, study, and entertaining opposing views. Authentic Judaism does not judge, and has tolerance for other approaches and religious thought. What a drastic departure from our Christian experience, where we were taught that people of different faiths have no place in Heaven. It was refreshing to be able to freely challenge and to dig deeper into the Torah for answers.

Because we've never been satisfied with merely attending a weekly service, Calvin and I fully immersed ourselves in spiritual study, which involved taking advantage of classes and other program offerings through Chabad Columbus, observing Jews in the shul and in their homes, and picking the brains of anyone who would let us. Thankfully, there were a number of generous individuals who would do just that. Rebbetzin Kaltmann taught a weekly women's parasha class that I started attending right away, and together, we attended Rabbi Kaltmann's Thursday parasha class. We also attended some of his more formal courses through the Rohr Jewish Learning Institute (JLI).

Rabbi Levy Andrusier, another Chabad Columbus pillar, taught JLI classes in the Jewish community and conducted more intimate classes at his home that we attended. He was always willing to answer any question we had. The warmth, patience, and encouragement he and his wife, Aviva, showed us forged an enduring friendship. Being frequent guests at their Shabbos and Yom Tov tables enabled me to see the practical application of Jewish laws including kashrus. Watching a kosher kitchen in operation is a much richer learning experience than trying to interpret a book on the subject. Without this exposure, assimilation would have been much slower and more difficult.

Our first "real" Shabbos meal was with the Kaltmanns. Unbeknownst to us, our new friend Cindy had been encouraging the rabbi and his wife to invite us for Shabbos dinner. Rabbi Kaltmann would respond with, "When the time is right." He is wise and, before inviting us into his home with his family, he would make sure we were sincere in our intentions. We have learned that trust is an important theme with Jews, and Rabbi Kaltmann needed to trust us before the time would be right to share a Shabbos meal with us. After attending services and classes every week for several weeks, he must have been convinced our intentions were genuine, because we received an invitation to dinner.

What a stunning experience! Their Shabbos table was graced with gorgeous table settings, platters of sumptuous delicacies, and Esther's melt-in-your-mouth *challah* (special braided bread eaten on Sabbath and Jewish holidays).

The Kaltmanns were as welcoming to us in their home as they had been at Chabad. They have a special talent for making each guest feel important.

More striking even than the food and the ceremony was how the

Kaltmanns interacted with their inquisitive and outgoing children. Rabbi Kaltmann has a special way of including the children through singing and storytelling. He asked questions of the children to engage them in the conversation. We benefited from the discussion as much as, if not more than, the children did. This was a means of acquiring more knowledge, not only about the parasha, but also about halacha, and especially as it pertains to observing Shabbos.

After the ice was broken with the Kaltmanns' invitation, we had invitations almost every week from the Kaltmanns and several other families. Dr. Larry and Mrs. Meryl Weprin and their family made an incredible effort to encourage us along our path that eventually led to conversion. They were fascinated by the story of how we came to be where we were. In fact, it was the Weprins who suggested we write this book, and Meryl came up with the title. Several years later, under the *chuppah* (wedding canopy), Dr. Weprin would give one of the *brachos* (blessings). Along the way, at some of the more difficult moments during the conversion process, the Weprins were there to lend support. The very day after we moved into the Jewish community, the Weprins showed up with a delicious turkey dinner to welcome us to our new home.

We even made friends with a woman visiting from Israel. Andee made *aliyah* (immigration of Jews to Israel) several years before, and told us she was now living in Netanya, a beautiful coastal city in the Northern Central District. In that short conversation, she extended an offer to stay with her if we were ever in Israel. I found it remarkable that after such a brief meeting she would offer to open her home to us, virtual strangers. And she was sincere; this was not just the frivolous offer that some people make, never expecting the recipient to accept.

While attending Chabad Columbus, someone suggested we visit Crown Heights, a Brooklyn neighborhood with a large Hasidic population and the headquarters of the Chabad-Lubavitch Hasidic movement. Given our obvious thirst for knowledge and involvement at Chabad Columbus, it made sense that we would be interested in learning about different sects of Judaism.

Viewing a Hasidic community from the inside offered a better understanding of the culture, daily activities, and holiday observance.

I planned a three-day trip during *Succos* (commonly translated Feast of Tabernacles, a biblical Jewish holiday celebrated on the 15th day of the seventh month, Tishrei). This would include a day of sightseeing on our own, Shabbos, and an organized Hasidic Walking Tour through the neighborhood. During our first day of exploration, we were admiring the hundreds of *sukkahs* (temporary structures for dwelling) that had been built for the holiday. It was dramatic to see an entire community observing the sukkah ritual, not something we would expect to see in Columbus. During the Succos holiday, one of the commandments is to take a *lulav* (branch of a palm tree bundled with other branches) and an *etrog* (citron) and wave them in a specific manner while reciting a blessing. Chabad is known for its outreach, and its youth were encouraged to go into the streets to invite other Jews to partake. While Calvin and I were sitting on a bench resting our feet, taking in all the wonders, Chabad youth had flooded the street and were approaching the passers-by, asking if they were Jewish. If the answer was "Yes," they would ask if they would like to perform the *mitzvah* (a commandment). It is a joyous act, and was so fun for us to watch.

We witnessed one child receive a nasty rejection from a bystander, and Calvin jumped right up to go lend support to the boy. Calvin told him that he appreciated what he was doing, and so did Hashem. Calvin also told him what he was doing was a *kiddush Hashem* (sanctification of G-d's name) and to stay a proud Jew. He is such a natural with kids and knows exactly how to relate to them.

We stayed with a local rabbi who had advertised a room for rent on a Chabad website I visited. I was clear when I called that we were non-Jews but would be visiting to learn about the Jewish community there, and that we had reserved spots on the Walking Tour. While it might have been overkill in some circumstances, I always felt strongly that we should be totally transparent about our religious status to avoid any assumptions that could lead to awkward moments or feelings of distrust. I never wanted there to be the slightest hint that this was our intention.

The rabbi welcomed us with open arms to rent his room, to eat meals in his sukkah, and even took us to his shul, Congregation Bais Shmuel, then led by the famous Rabbi Y.Y. Jacobson. On Shabbos, he also escorted us to the Chabad-Lubavitch Hasidic movement headquarters, famously referred to as "770" for its location at 770 Eastern Parkway. Near the end of our visit, we were enjoying a meal in his sukkah, and all of a sudden he asked, "Who is G-d's son?" We sat there dumbfounded wondering why he was asking us this question. We were not sure how to respond, so we sat in silence. He proceeded to read out of the Chumash Exodus 4:22: "... so said Hashem, my firstborn son is Israel." To this day, we discuss and ponder what might have been his intention in pointing this out. Maybe it was just a point of educating us; we will probably never know for sure.

He and his wife were exceedingly kind to us during our stay. They made us feel like welcome guests even though we were obviously outsiders. The rabbi even made sure Calvin did not have anything in his pockets when walking to the shul on Shabbos, since carrying is a Shabbos violation.

Going to 770 for Shabbos was a magnificent experience. It was packed with several thousand people. The women's section was on the upper floors, while the men's section was on the main floor. Seeing fathers and sons davening and singing together was beautiful and emotional. When they discovered that I was a visitor, the women made room for me in the front row so I could see what was happening on the main floor below. They helped me with the *siddur* (Jewish prayer book), turning pages for me and making sure I was on the right page. Shabbos at 770 was a spiritually elevating experience for both of us.

Because it was Succos, the community threw a huge street party on m*otzei Shabbos* (the evening after Shabbos). A street was blocked off, and the air was filled with aromas of pizza and popcorn. A band played Jewish tunes on a makeshift stage, and hundreds of men danced with their children. Families were together. People were smiling and happy. We felt much joy as we stood on the street corner and watched the sights.

Sunday was the culmination of our trip to Crown Heights with the Hasidic Walking Tour. This tour included another visit to Chabad-Lubavitch World Headquarters, a tour of the Main Synagogue, the Rebbe's Library, an extensive and educational tour of a mikveh, and lunch at a local deli. Rabbi Beryl Epstein taught us about Hasidic customs, culture and lifestyles. We learned of the origins of the Hasidic movement, which was founded in 1734 by the Baal Shem Tov in Europe. This tour was amazing and inspiring, giving us an up-close-and-personal look into a spiritual and cultural world few outsiders take the time to discover. For us, it was a real privilege. Rabbi Epstein shared deep insight, humor, historical perspectives, and enthusiasm. He was willing to answer any questions posed to him, of which there were many, especially concerning the mikveh and family purity issues, a subject not known about or understood by the non-Jewish world.

This short trip to Crown Heights was especially meaningful for us. We added an aspect to our Jewish base of knowledge not readily available in Ohio, and were very touched by the beauty of the Crown Heights community.

Our religious knowledge grew by leaps and bounds over the two years we attended Chabad, the main difference coming from the focus on halacha and proper observance that was missing from our independent study. We were learning from traditional Jewish sources for the first time, instead of materials that put a Christian spin on anything Jewish. Several families had befriended us and welcomed us into their lives, allowing for practical observation, further enhancing our understanding of how to integrate G-d's laws into everyday life.

We had continued with our independent Shabbos group for about a year after visiting Chabad for the first time. It was obvious our beliefs were evolving, differently than some in the group, and people were attending less consistently for various reasons. It was a mutual decision by the remaining members to officially disband. A couple of families went to the local messianic congregation, and several families eventually converted. That was the end of any non-Jewish religious affiliation for Calvin and me. The group served an essential purpose in each member's journey and was incredibly fulfilling, but it had run its course and everyone felt it was time to move on.

It was at Chabad Columbus that we eventually made the leap, deciding to convert, and Rabbi Kaltmann agreed to sponsor us. Esther Kaltmann graciously committed her time to teach me once a week at her home. We covered many topics: davening, kosher kitchen, laws of Shabbos, kashrus, how to make challah, special concerns of the *Pesach* (Passover) kitchen, and many other important aspects of Jewish life. These learning sessions were intense and invaluable in preparing me for conversion. I am forever grateful for the opportunity to learn from such a special Rebbetzin.

We knew converting meant we would have to move to a Jewish community, within walking distance of a shul. Unfortunately, Chabad Columbus is located in a very affluent area and was not an option for us. So, after two years, we said goodbye to our regular attendance and involvement, but took our lasting friendships and unforgettable experiences with us into our future Jewish lives, where we would ultimately be having our own "real" Shabbos.

CHAPTER 15

MOTHER-DAUGHTER TRIP TO ISRAEL: VOLUNTEERS FOR ISRAEL

My mom began an annual mother-daughter weekend tradition with my sisters and me almost 20 years ago. The five of us would leave our husbands, kids, and the rest of our responsibilities behind to spend a weekend holed up playing board games, eating junk food, and laughing hysterically. These weekends were meaningful for the quality time focused on each other, and for the recharging effect it had on each of us, before we returned to our busy lives. Over the years, we created mountains of delightful memories on visits throughout Ohio to Amish Country, Kelly's Island, Cincinnati, The Wilds, Chagrin Falls, and Maumee Bay State Park.

Having one daughter and five sons, I find carving out special mother-daughter time vital to nurturing my close relationship with Hannah. We ladies are outnumbered in a large family of boys and men, and we feel it necessary to schedule "girl time." In 2010, Hannah was 15 and I was ready for a return visit to Israel. A bit more than the traditional weekends my mom would plan with us, but what better way to bond with my daughter than to show her a place I love? We were going to Israel.

Rather than a purely relaxing, sight-seeing trip, we decided to look for an opportunity to do something that offered an insider's view of Israel, and the opportunity to meet people from all over the world who share our love and concern for the country. I found a program called Volunteers for Israel whose mission it is to connect Americans to Israel through volunteer service. It is a nonprofit, non-political, and non-sectarian organization with a long history of service to the people of Israel, and it sounded perfect to us.

Established in 1982, during the first war with Lebanon, the program was started due to a lack of people to harvest crops. Men and women were being called into reserve service to defend the country's northern flank, leaving no one to work the fields. To avoid economic devastation, Israeli General Aharon Davidi sent emissaries to the United States to recruit volunteers. Six hundred Americans joined the cause and were so moved by their experience, they set up regional groups throughout the U.S. to continue the partnership with Israeli military and civilian organizations.

After a lengthy and involved application process and travel arrangements shrouded in mystery, we arrived at our destination for our two-week project. For security reasons, we were not told of our assignment location until we landed at Ben Gurion airport near Tel Aviv. We learned our group of thirty volunteers was to be dispatched to an Israeli Defense Forces (IDF) medical supply base, which serves as the hub for the entire country. We would be performing non-combat civilian support duties, such as preparing supply kits to be sent overseas as part of Israel's massive emergency aid programs. Soldiers, base employees, and other volunteers worked side-by-side to help shoulder Israel's defense burden.

Each morning, wearing our IDF-issued fatigues, we began with breakfast with the soldiers, followed by the flag-raising. Throughout the weeks we were on the base, volunteers took turns raising the flag. I was honored to be chosen one morning to conduct the ceremonious flag-raising, enthusiastically exhibiting my support for the soldiers and for the State of Israel.

After the flag-raising, everyone would go to their appointed work areas. Hannah and I worked in a warehouse, standing hunched over long tables of medicines, bandages, and IV-tubing that we would pack into kits. A reprieve from the hunching, but no less taxing on our backs, we intermittently unloaded boxes of provisions from the large pallets others brought into the warehouse. August in Israel is nothing like August in Ohio. It was brutally hot, nearing 115 degrees on most days; and although the warehouse was air-conditioned, it was not sufficient to provide relief, with workers constantly opening the large doors. I imagine it was worse for some of the men who were carrying materials from one place to another out in the blazing sun.

Evenings were spent participating with our group in cultural and educational activities. We learned some basic Hebrew, geography, and about life in Israel. The highlight for me was having a high-ranking IDF sergeant speak to us and convey his deep appreciation for the work we were doing. He made us feel that our work was a significant contribution to the country. One night, the base commander told us that in the present year, on our base alone, volunteers saved 10 million shekels (equivalent to $2.8 million at the time of this writing) by eliminating the need for the IDF to call up salaried reservists and by fixing old equipment instead of buying new. It was rewarding to hear that our work made a real difference.

After a full and exhausting day, we would retire to our mercifully air-conditioned barracks to rest up for more important and backbreaking work the next day. The barracks were comfortable, but the description of "somewhat primitive" held true for the bathrooms. Hannah and I shared accommodations at the start, but then she made friends with some other volunteers and went to stay with some that were her age. Our group was truly multicultural, about 80% Jewish and 20% non-Jewish, ranging in age from sixteen into their seventies. Many were returning volunteers, coming back because of the deep personal satisfaction they gained from their efforts. It was rewarding to see people from all over the world who shared this love for Israel, and who would do everything they could to support and help this tiny, great country.

The weekends, spent off base, were ours to do with as we pleased. Most of the volunteers went to a youth hostel near Tel Aviv, but Hannah and I were interested in more adventure. We decided to go to the northern part of the country and visit Tiveria (Tiberias), a beautiful and vibrant city on the western shore of the Sea of Galilee, and Beit She'an, one of the oldest cities in Israel, where the Harod and Jordan valleys meet. We were awed by the beautiful, unique building and private pool overlooking the Gilboa mountains. The expansive view from our window was breathtaking.

The weekend went by too quickly, filled with shopping, eating, walking along the boardwalk in Tiveria, and reflecting on the work we had done that week. And, of course, resting up for our return to the base. Hannah's appetite for seeing more of Israel whetted, we eagerly returned to the base to complete our mission, so we could get on with more exploration of the country.

Our second week consisted of more hard labor, but was broken up with a field trip to Zichron Ya'acov. We traveled by bus to this beautiful, quaint town built at the top of the Carmel mountain range. The streets are paved with stone and lined with charming restaurants, art galleries, coffee shops, and stores. That day we also visited the Rothschild Gardens, known in Israel as Ramat Hanadiv, where many ecological advancements have been incorporated into the buildings and systems. Our last stop before returning to the base, the Tishbi Winery, offered a guided tour complete with an explanation of the wine-making process. Sampling the wine and gourmet chocolate was a luxurious reprieve from our duties.

We finished the second week of our volunteering, and with heavy hearts, bade farewell to our new friends. My first two trips to Israel had been for sightseeing. This time, deciding to volunteer and being immersed in a central part of the life of the nation, was a totally different experience. Living rough along with the young soldiers – living in the same types of barracks, eating the same food, working the same hours on some of the same jobs – was a small but significant way of experiencing what nearly every Israeli youth goes through, as military or other national service is required in Israel.

Wanting to make the most of our mother-daughter Israel encounter, Hannah and I included a week for uninterrupted tourism in our vacation. When we completed our volunteer commitment, we left the base for an apartment I had rented in Jerusalem. We quickly unpacked and set out for the *Kotel*, commonly referred to as the Western Wall, the holiest place Jews are allowed to pray. I had been there twice previously, but it was wonderful to see Hannah's reaction to the history and sanctity of this place.

The next day, we saw the Bible come alive during a tour of the City of David. Not surprisingly, Hannah's favorite part was sloshing through Hezekiah's Tunnel. We spent several hours at the site exploring the remains of King Herod's palace.

Another day was spent touring Masada and the Dead Sea. We left the plateau of Masada to go a short distance down the road to the Ein Gedi Spa at the Dead Sea. There, we spent several hours on the beach floating in the Dead Sea, smearing the famous Dead Sea black mud all over ourselves and lying in the sun, savoring the beautiful weather and surroundings. Although different from spas back home, Ein Gedi has the same relaxing and refreshing effect. The place is so unreal that it makes it hard to believe this is the same earth that Ohio inhabits. The day ended with an exciting camel ride for Hannah.

The number one thing on Hannah's to-do list was snorkeling with the dolphins in the Red Sea; so the next day, we boarded the bus for the ride to Eilat, a resort and port town as far south as you can go in Israel. Dolphin Reef allows visitors to observe the Black Sea bottlenose dolphins and their babies born at the site, either from the floating piers or during a guided swim. Hannah, opting for the swim, donned her snorkeling gear and set out for her adventure.

The holding area for the dolphins is a large, natural cove, bordered with underwater nets that blend in to the environmental surroundings. It is a gorgeous place to observe and interact with the dolphins while they maintain their daily routine of hunting, playing, courting and socializing within their ecological habitat.

Spending so much time visiting the ancient ruins, seaside spas, and biblical locales can make Israel feel a million miles from the U.S., where nothing of the like can be found. But, back in Jerusalem, there is a lively area, crowded with locals and tourists doing the things that make our two countries feel much less dissimilar. Ben Yehuda Street is a pedestrian mall replete with eateries, shops, street performers, and musicians. It is one of Jerusalem's prime hangouts for people of all ages. I had been there on both of my previous visits, but wanted Hannah to see that life in Israel is not so vastly different in many ways than what she sees in America.

On Saturday nights, after Shabbat, the shops and cafes begin to turn on lights and open their doors, performers take their places on sidewalks, and revelers wander the streets, filling Ben Yehuda with buzzing activity. Hannah and I mingled with the locals and other tourists and found a favorite place to eat called Big Apple Pizza. It was another dimension of the country that we were glad to have experienced.

The last stop on our near-perfect trip was in Netanya, another resort city with sandy beaches and cultural attractions. Prior to our visit, I had contacted Andee, the Israeli visitor we'd met at Chabad Columbus, to let her know Hannah and I were coming to Israel and would like to take her up on the kind offer of a place to stay. Andee graciously shared her home with us for several days before we had to return to America.

This trip provided so many enriching opportunities for the two of us and, for me, was capped with meeting a very special person who has become a very important part of my life. At a friend's suggestion, I had read a book called *My Sister the Jew,* written by Ms. Ahuvah Gray. The book recounts the true story of an African-American minister, a descendant of sharecroppers, who chose to exchange the American Dream for a dream of her own – to follow the courageous path of the convert, eventually becoming a Torah-observant Jew. I was fascinated with her story, and thought I could learn something from her.

I reached out to her via e-mail and told her that my daughter Hannah and I were coming to Israel on a volunteer trip, and would love to meet her. Ahuvah quickly agreed, and when we arrived at her tiny apartment, a beautiful, intelligent, articulate, and vivacious woman met us with a big smile and a warm hug. We visited for several hours, and she gave me several autographed books. Making Ahuvah's acquaintance has deeply affected my life. To date, we speak on the phone nearly every day except Shabbat, and we are truly soul sisters. I have visited her on all of my subsequent trips to Israel. Ahuvah is definitely one of the clear and obvious signs I prayed for as we started out on our spiritual journey.

I believe this trip had a profound impact not just on me, but on Hannah as well. She and Isaiah, because of their ages, had been more involved in our journey than the older kids, so naturally had more understanding of what was happening. But as we were deciding to change our religious affiliation, we were not expecting our children to follow suit. This was our journey; they will have their own. Being in Israel with me gave Hannah deeper insights into Calvin's and my transition and our love of the Holy Land. She was given a first-hand view of what we were experiencing which, I believe, made it easier for her to accept.

The trip also served its purpose of strengthening our mother-daughter bond. Beyond that, it was incredibly fulfilling to us both to be able to help Israel in a tangible way, by supporting the Israel Defense Forces. I am so blessed to have been able to experience Israel with my daughter. A few months after we returned from the trip, Hannah's English teacher left this message for me:

Hi Jeri, this is Frank from Tree of Life. I have Hannah in English class and she did a really nice job this morning. She led our devotionals. We have first-period devotionals every day. She talked about her trip to Israel and how, as difficult as some of the people have it over there, they really seem to look at the best parts of life. And then she said that is what you tell her all the time, to think about the good. And anyway, it was a real nice devotional and it got everybody positive for the day. I want to let you know how much I enjoy having her in class and you would have been proud of her today...

I was proud of her. I am proud of her. Every day.

CHAPTER 16

THE DECISION TO CONVERT

Rather than a single moment of revelation, the decision to become Orthodox Jews was a gradual awareness brought about by several catalysts. Occasionally, other Chabad members would ask us if it was our intention to convert, and some of our friends from our home group had begun their own conversions, effectively planting the seed of possibility. As we settled into our place at Chabad, we faced the choice of either converting or remaining righteous Gentiles and observing the Noachide commandments. The latter we thought would not fulfill us spiritually; and after eight years of investigation, conversion ideas were starting to sprout.

We began to hypothesize about what conversion would mean for us. We would ask each other, "If we converted, how would we maintain a kosher kitchen with non-Jewish kids still at home?" and "If we converted, how would we navigate family gatherings like our annual family picnic or visits to Calvin's New Jersey family?" We were even casually looking for living accommodations near Chabad, knowing we would have to eliminate driving to shul to keep Shabbos.

Over the years, we had incorporated many of the required observances into our lives: I was dressing more conservatively in skirts, we were covering our heads on Shabbos, and were stocking our kitchen with kosher foods. But the reality of going from mostly observant to always and forever observant was overwhelming. We had to consider the permanence of the changes we would have to make and how it would affect our children, family and friends. Observing as a non-Jew was very different from living as a Jew.

Calvin was used to regularly attending high school football games as part of Football Friday Night. He was expected, as an Ohio State Buckeye Football alumnus, to take part in alumni events, like celebrity golf outings and game attendance, that usually occurred on Saturdays. He loved his role in the football community, and the thought of removing himself from that felt like giving up a part of his identity. Calvin felt he would have to sacrifice more than I, and was not willing to take any action toward conversion until he was ready to embrace it fully and willingly. Permanently.

For my part, I felt that Calvin didn't fully appreciate the significance of the changes I would have to make. I would have to completely eliminate shorts and pants from my wardrobe, which meant I would have to learn to do my 30-mile bike rides in a skirt. I was going to have to cover my hair all the time, not just on Shabbos, which I wondered how I would do within the confines of the law office dress code. I had never worn a wig before, and the idea seemed strange. I had to figure out how to modify some of our favorite family meals that contained meat mixed with dairy, and do the grocery shopping to maintain dietary rules without causing the kids to stage a revolt.

The considerations were no small matter for either of us. We were told once (not by a rabbi!), "After you convert, you can do whatever you want," indicating we didn't need to be observant after we achieved conversion. Although it was meant by this non-observant Jew to provide reassurance, I was angered by it. Calvin and I are not the type of people to do things halfway. If we are going to do something, we are going to do it the right way, with total commitment.

I eventually came around to the conversion idea sooner than Calvin. Through practice, I started to realize the changes would not be easy, but would be manageable with Hashem's guidance. Calvin continued to contemplate how he would make the lifestyle changes necessary to live as an Orthodox Jew.

Calvin's mom had told him once that she saw a "glow" on him when he was born that she didn't understand. She had already passed on by the time we were going through this deliberation, but she spoke to him in a dream. She said, "I know what that glow that I saw on you when you were born is now.

You have a Jewish *neshama* (soul). Go and finish your course." Carol didn't know Hebrew so Calvin was shocked to hear her say these words and viewed it as a true sign from Hashem. After this dream, he told me he was ready to convert, and we took the next step. Though conversion involves many large and small sacrifices, we saw that they would be well worth the fulfillment we would get from making them.

An Orthodox conversion requires a rabbinical sponsor. Approval by the Beis Din cannot be gained until the rabbis are completely convinced that candidates have pure motivations, have a thorough understanding of Shabbos observance and kashrut and are willing and able to live and thrive within the Jewish community. Even after this, there are requirements that the candidates complete several rituals, such as circumcision, mikveh immersion, selecting a Hebrew name, and, for us, a Jewish wedding, to recommit ourselves in our new religion.

We approached Rabbi Kaltmann expressing our desire to convert, and asked him if he would consider sponsoring us. He said he was convinced of our sincerity and commitment, since he had observed us attending every week for every class, every service, always early, and willing to help in any way we could. He agreed to contact the Beis Din to set up an initial interview. He also offered to meet with us after the weekly kiddush (the communal gathering after Sabbath morning services) to study halacha.

We had been studying now for eight years and practicing much of what we learned, but incredibly, we still did not know enough about living as Jews. Our studies shifted from general beliefs to more intensive examination of the *Shulchan Aruch* (Code of Jewish Law) and took many forms – online classes, regular classes, lectures, and personal mentoring. We were eager to learn everything we could for our own benefit, but also to demonstrate seriousness in becoming Jews to the rabbis at the Beis Din.

I became acquainted with Aish HaTorah. Their website is extensive and contains commentaries on the weekly parasha, Judaism 101, current issues in Israel, spirituality, and so much more. My favorite part of the Aish website was Jewish Pathways Advanced Learning, offering many study courses. I dove head first into courses including Jewish History, Laws of Blessings, Laws of Shabbat, and Daily Living. I had more time than Calvin to dedicate to study, so I would digest the material and share it with him. We listened to many *shiurim* (study sessions usually led by a rabbi) on the Chabad website together.

The conversion process is not easy and it is not fast. We knew we were going to need support beyond the rabbi's sponsorship and coaching to be successful. We asked Hashem to open doors that needed to be opened and to bring people into our lives that would help and support us during this transition period. And then we met Yerachmiel from Michigan. As with most first meetings, we were oblivious to how significant this man would be in our lives or what a personal investment he would make in our future.

Yerachmiel was visiting Chabad as a special cantor for the High Holy Days services. His voice was like honey, and his davening was beautiful. We felt compelled to compliment his heartfelt davening afterward and, during the conversation, we agreed to meet for dinner before he returned home. We shared our story with him, and he was so moved that he generously offered to conduct Skype sessions with us to prepare us for meetings with the Beis Din and ultimately with our conversion.

For over a year, he prepared extensive outlines for us to guide our studies between meetings, and clarified our questions or quizzed us during the weekly Skype sessions. When we later showed the outlines to the rabbis of the Beis Din, they were extremely impressed with Yerachmiel's work and the depth of his teaching. We studied the brachos for three months, and then moved on to the halachos of Shabbos.

By 2011, Judaism had enhanced our lives to the point that we were completely clear in our decision to formally adopt this religion, convert and become Jews. All signs pointed to this as our destination. We felt we could not have spiritual fulfillment in any other way. The more we researched, the more Judaism made sense to us. Judaism brings intellect and reason to our faith and defines actions that lead to self-improvement, whereas Christianity focuses mainly on blind faith. When we leave this world and stand before G-d, we don't think He will ask us what we believed. He will ask us, "What did you do with the life I gave you?" Christianity emphasizes being saved or not saved and making it to Heaven, whereas Judaism stresses the here and now. Judaism offers such a directed and beautiful way of life. It cultivates an attitude of gratitude, and gives purpose and direction to all areas of life. It concentrates on making the world a better place. Judaism has a blessing for almost everything – waking up in the morning, sights, smells, natural wonders, food, weather events, you name it. Nothing is taken for granted. This is a constant reminder of G-d's presence. This is why we wanted to be Jews.

The Pesach after we met, Yerachmiel and his wife, Chayala, invited us to their home in Michigan for the two Seders. We had never attended an authentic Seder, as the ones our home group held were not attended by anyone Jewish, and this occurred before we had an opportunity to experience a Seder at Chabad. This was another incredible opportunity to learn, both through conversation and by observing how Pesach is celebrated in an observant family. And, the food! Chayala prepared the most elegant table, laden with traditional dishes, Seder plates, place settings, flowers, and the nicest personal touch of unique name cards.

This would become a tradition for us – to travel to Michigan for the first two days of Pesach. We went the second year to them as non-Jews and, finally, in 2013, we would sit at our dear friends' table as Jews.

CHAPTER 17

ISRAEL WITH CALVIN | 2012

After we had begun the conversion process, I felt it was time for my devoted husband to experience the Holy Land for himself, so Calvin and I began planning our visit to Israel together in November 2012. I could not wait to show him this beautiful country and its incredibly moving biblical sites, to introduce him to the people of Israel, and to see the wonder I knew would be in his eyes. I also looked forward to sharing the experience of visiting new places and meeting new people together.

Israel is a small country, about the size of New Jersey, spanning 263 miles from north to south and 71 miles across at its widest point, and we planned to cover a good portion of it in our two-week visit. Ten days of our trip would be spent in and around Jerusalem, followed by shorter stays in Tiveria, Tsfat, Masada and Netanya. It was going to be a challenge for us to strike a balance between fitting in all of the stops on our itinerary and allowing time to absorb and relish the grandeur, not to mention travel between locations.

Unfortunately, just as our plane landed in Jerusalem, things were heating up in Gaza, and a conflict, later known as Operation Pillar of Defense, erupted. While I had come to expect to see soldiers in the streets from my previous visits, and we were both well aware of the unrest present in the area, we were not entirely prepared to witness people running to bomb shelters when the sirens sounded. Unsettling as it was, this unforeseen skirmish did not derail our enthusiasm, and caused only minor disruptions to our schedule.

Jerusalem, with its concentration of biblical sites, is a place we could have easily spent our entire trip and still not seen everything it has to offer. We visited the Western Wall (Kotel), Hezekiah's Tunnel, the Old Jewish Quarter, and the City of David. We ventured further out of the city to the Valley of Elah and the city of Modi'in, where we attended the Footsteps of the Maccabees tour. The Maccabees tour was a replacement activity in lieu of visiting Kever Rochel (the burial place of our Matriarch, Rachel) and Hevron (Hebron) due to safety concerns related to Operation Pillar of Defense.

The City of David tour offers the option to walk through the dry tunnel or the water tunnel. Choosing the water tunnel means walking where water has flowed since the time of the prophets. King Hezekiah decided to protect the city's water by diverting its flow deep into the city with an impressive 1,750-foot tunnel through the mountain. Calvin wanted to experience the effect of being physically close to what he had read in the Bible, essentially to *feel* the history, so he opted for the water tunnel. The average height of the tunnel is not even six feet, and it is barely two feet wide. This required him to stoop to avoid hitting his head, and his shoulders brushed both sides as he walked. He never thought himself claustrophobic but, when he emerged, he wanted to get as far out in the open as he could. It reminded me of how I felt after my hike down Mount Arbel on my first trip to Israel. Today, we can laugh about our terrifying experiences, mine caused by my too-small stature and his by his too-large stature.

I had done the tunnel walk on a previous visit, but we were able to participate in a tour that was new to both of us while we were in the City of David. The Temple Mount Ascent tour was recently added due to recent excavations, and we could now walk the ancient streets of Jerusalem. The most exciting part of the tour was seeing the impressive foundation stones of the Western Wall at the foot of the Temple Mount. One of the stones is 41 feet long, 14 feet high, and weighs over 500 metric tons. What an incredible sight! Being able to walk on the same road where the Jewish pilgrims walked 2,000 years ago gave us a sense of awe and respect.

When we took our seats on the Footsteps of the Maccabees tour bus at the Prima Kings Hotel, my husband said, "Honey, guess who's sitting behind us?" I turned around and there sat Lana and her husband, Gary, friends from Columbus and congregants of the shul we attended. We began to understand what people meant when they said Israel is such a small country! We never expected to see anyone from back home. We had a nice day with them and made plans to meet them the next day for lunch.

For some time leading up to our trip, I had been listening to the Yishai Fleisher radio program. Besides being a radio show host, Yishai is the international spokesman for the Jewish community in Hevron, and a writer for many publications that cover Israeli current events. I emailed Yishai several months before the trip and told him Calvin and I would be in Israel and would love to meet him and his wife, Malkah. He agreed to coordinate a meeting once we arrived in Israel. He must have been excited by my request, because he mentioned our communication the following week on his radio show.

After a brief initial phone call when we first arrived, we did not hear back from Yishai in the next several days. We assumed that he either was out reporting on Operation Pillar of Defense or had been called up for reserve duty. I was greatly disappointed, but Calvin reassured me that it was all Hashem's will, and if we were supposed to meet Yishai, it would happen.

A few days later, we took the light rail from our apartment to the Chut Shel Chessed Yeshiva to see and hear one of our favorite rabbis, Rabbi Lazer Brody, from Breslev Israel. Breslov is a branch of Hasidic Judaism founded by Rebbe Nachman, a great-grandson of the Baal Shem Tov, founder of Hasidism. Their main messages are emunah and serving Hashem with *simcha* (happiness). They also espouse *hitbodedut* (personal communication with G-d, a very Jewish kind of meditation) for at least an hour a day.

I sat in the women's section with a friend. After a few minutes of his shiur, Rabbi Brody called out to someone on the men's side to give a report of the conflict. I thought I heard him address the man by the name "Yishai" but couldn't be entirely sure I had heard correctly. And, even if I did hear correctly, he couldn't possibly be *the* Yishai I had been hoping to meet, could he?

After the shiur was over, I stood beside the men's section waiting for Calvin. I told him I thought maybe the man who gave the update was Yishai Fleisher, and asked him to go ask the man if he was indeed Yishai. He did, and sure enough, it was he! Yishai said that with everything going on in Israel with the Gaza conflict, he felt he needed an extra dose of emunah, and came to hear Rabbi Brody. Yishai was equally excited that we had come to the same place, and in spite of everything going on, Hashem saw fit to have us meet. Such an amazing example of *hashgacha pratis* (Divine providence).

We met Yishai and his wife, Malkah, at Café Café at Mamilla Mall the next day for what we expected would be just a nice lunch and an opportunity to get to know them. They were intensely interested in hearing about our journey to Judaism. After a delicious meal during which we shared a bit about our spiritual journey with them, Yishai pulled out a microphone and said, "You have to tell our listeners your story!" A jolt of alarm swept through my body at the mention of any public speaking. Conversely, Calvin is unfazed by public speaking and accepted the spontaneous request without missing a beat. We did the radio interview, and I was relieved to feel my nerves quieting as we settled into the rhythm of the interview.

Shortly after our meeting with Yishai, we traveled north to Tiveria. The surrounding mountains and expansive lake views are spectacular, giving the feeling of being cozily cradled by the landscape.

The Yigal Allon Promenade, a restaurant-lined boardwalk along the Kinneret, is a lively area, great for people-watching or for leisurely walks.

As we strolled the boardwalk, we saw a sign advertising motor boat rental. This was a leg of our trip that was less structured, with fewer tours and excursions, so we thought, "Why not?" and set out for a thirty-minute boat ride. The sun was high and bright in a deep blue sky, and as we cruised across the lake, the boat swayed and rocked us gently, comforting us in our introspection. It was beautiful to relax and reflect on all we had seen and experienced together over the last several days. We had been feverishly running from one site to the next, not wanting to miss anything, and this served as a necessary break to rebalance our scale and let everything sink in.

After our short stay in Tiveria, we made our way further north to Tsfat (Safed), a magnificent mountaintop town that joins Jerusalem, Hevron and Tiveria in its designation as one of the four holy cities in Israel. Tsfat is an ancient Galilean city wrapped in mysticism. Whether it was the fresh, clean mountain air, the holy significance or the altitude, I can only describe it as a heavenly experience. We ended up loving Tsfat so much that we cancelled our next stop and decided to stay another two nights.

Rabbi Kaltmann, from the Chabad shul that gave us our start in Judaism, arranged for us to have Shabbat dinner with Rabbi Mordechai "Big Mo" Siev, who is the Director of Ascent of Tsfat. He and his wife were warm and welcoming, and we shared two delicious meals with them. Prior to Shabbat dinner, we enjoyed a Kabbalat Shabbat service at Ascent, which was a very joyful ushering in of Shabbat full of singing and dancing.

Ascent of Tsfat offers various classes throughout the day on subjects such as Torah, *Kabbalah* (mystical interpretation of the Bible) and *Hasidut* (the teachings, interpretations, and various practices of Judaism as articulated by the Hasidic movement), as well as walking tours of Tsfat. We took advantage of both the classes and a walking tour, so we could continue our learning while seeing firsthand several beautiful synagogues and some ancient Torah scrolls.

We spent several hours one day investigating Tsfat's ancient cemetery. The inscriptions reveal the names of the city's sages and mystics, most notably the Arizal, Rabbi Isaac Luria, considered the greatest Kabbalist of all time, who instituted the Kabbalat Shabbat. Also located here, near the upper entrance to the old cemetery, is the Ari's Mikveh, built on a natural spring, in which tradition says the Ari would dip. It is customary for male visitors to partake, but because we were not yet Jewish, Calvin would have to wait until a future trip to experience the mikveh for himself.

A standout among the number of services we attended while in Israel was the *Havdalah* service (marking the end of Shabbat) at The House of Love and Prayer, a synagogue where the melodies of Rabbi Shlomo Carlebach filled our souls with joy. The House of Love and Prayer is a tiny synagogue in the Old City of Tsfat, and it was filled to overflowing with locals and tourists on this day. As with all Orthodox synagogues, there are separate sections for men and women; and attendees who were able to squeeze in occupied every seat on both sides and stood shoulder to shoulder in every open space, bouncing and swaying to the rousing music. This service was unique to us in that it was musical with rocking guitars, flutes and drums, and it was a glorious way to say farewell to a most fulfilling Shabbat.

We have found throughout our integration into the Jewish community that devout Jews are well-connected to other Jews and always willing to make introductions to help converts build the support network needed to be successful. We know this was essential to our transition and eventual conversion. For every trip I made to Israel, including this one, friends and associates from Columbus gave me a number of contacts in Israel to meet. Each contact proved to be another warm welcome and another lifeline of our network of support.

On this visit to Tsfat, Ahuvah Gray thought we would enjoy meeting her friend, Rena, because she felt we had a lot in common. Rena suggested meeting for lunch at The Milano, an Italian-style café that would become one of our favorites. We sat upstairs where diners can enjoy watching the pedestrians on the street below. We found we did indeed have a lot in common: religious perspectives, political views, outlook on life. I appreciated Rena as a direct, forthright, kind and extremely knowledgeable woman. As soon as we got initial introductions out of the way, I knew we were instant friends.

Rena has lived in Tsfat since making aliyah in 1991. Originally from Calgary, Alberta, she made aliyah from Toronto where she had been living since 1983. She knows Israel, and she knows Tsfat. It was interesting to listen to her talk about that journey, as until this trip, Calvin and I had not given immigrating to Israel any consideration, and for the second time in as many weeks this topic had presented itself.

One of the questions Yishai had asked us during our radio interview was of our interest in making aliyah. We told him that, having not considered it before it would, no doubt, be a dilemma for us, because all of our children and grandchildren are in the U.S. It would be difficult to be so far away from them, and since our children are not Jewish, it seemed unlikely that they would ever live in Israel. Despite our lack of interest at this point, but with no pressure, Yishai suggested some communities in Israel that he thought might be a good fit for us, and that we should consider visiting on future trips. I wrote down the names of the communities he mentioned, not really thinking that we would ever really visit them.

In Rena, we had met someone who has family and community ties in her country of origin but still found a way to make aliyah work. She has no regrets, and is happily living as an Israeli citizen. In the moment, it was impossible for us to fathom that we would ever live in Israel, but these two conversations were likely the initial seeds of possibility. The planting of the seeds took place on this trip, but it would take more time before they would take root.

We left Tsfat to make the more than three-hour trip south to Masada, where we spent two nights at the hostel. Masada, built in the year 30 BCE by King Herod, is a fortress in the middle of the desert. The elaborate architecture is just amazing, and it is astonishing to envision ancient people building something so large and complex. You could easily spend the better part of a day exploring everything on this mountain.

The morning after we arrived, we set out for the fortress, which is perched atop an isolated rock plateau at the eastern end of the Judean Desert overlooking the Dead Sea. The views on top are magnificent and sweeping. Visitors can choose to hike up the snake path or take a cable car to the top. Calvin and I opted for the latter, feeling it would be safer. Those magnificent sweeping views must have ignited our bravery, because we decided to descend using the path.

The path is rocky, steep, narrow, and seems never-ending with twists and turns. It took us about 30 minutes to climb down, and our legs were burning from the effort. In spite of this, I do want to come back some day and hike up the snake path to watch the sunrise over the Dead Sea. I am told that this is a spectacular sight.

Our time at the fortress of Masada and other nearby-attractions was packed with physical activity. Our legs still tired from the hike down from the fortress, we went to Ein Gedi, a remarkable nature preserve right on the shores of the Dead Sea. We hiked to Nakhal David and Nakhal Arugot, spring-fed streams, which have water flowing through them year-round. We saw many plants and animals mentioned in the Tanakh here. We hiked the lower Nakhal David Stream trail that passes waterfalls and pools, leading to the stunning David Waterfall where David Hamelech took refuge when he was pursued by King Saul. We got chills just standing there at a base of the waterfall, marveling at the natural majesty and the biblical significance.

After hiking around Ein Gedi for several hours, we decided to go to the Dead Sea to rest our weary bodies. Truly, this is one of the most extraordinary places on earth, more than 400 meters below sea level, surrounded by the Mountains of Moab to the East and the Judean Mountains to the West. It has the distinction of being the lowest point on dry land in the world. The Dead Sea is more than nine times saltier than the ocean, making it dense enough to float without assistance, and many believe it has healing properties. In fact, it is considered one of the world's first health resorts, attracting visitors going back thousands of years.

Although many parts of the shore require an admission fee, there is a free public beach with a bus stop right in front, showers, and a changing room with lockers. We found out the hard way that free is not always best. Navigating down a steep decline to the beach was precarious, and even more arduous once you got there. Rather than the nice, sandy beach we had anticipated, large stones covered the shore, making our walk to the water look more like a lurching, spastic dance. Calvin ended up getting a nasty cut on one of his feet as he was exiting the water. While painful to have an open cut in the salty water, we relied on the vaunted healing powers of the Dead Sea. After a short ride back to the Masada Hostel and a quick bite to eat, we dove into bed to recover from the physically demanding day.

Our final stop was our friend Andee's home in Netanya. We enjoyed spending several tranquil days with her at her gorgeous beach house, where we met several of her friends, including Barry, Adele, Warren, Nadia, and Sue, with whom we enjoyed an extremely lovely Shabbat dinner. On future trips to Israel, we would always travel to Netanya to connect with these friends. It was a satisfying way to close our visit to the Holy Land together.

Leading up to the trip, Calvin did not seem very excited, and explained he didn't really know what to expect. He could not imagine it to be as life-changing as I insisted it was. Nevertheless, once he witnessed for himself the Bible coming to life at all the sacred sites, made new acquaintances to strengthen our Jewish social network, and observed new and different ways to practice Judaism, he said it just grabs hold of you. From the kosher restaurants to synagogues on every corner, the entire atmosphere is steeped in Jewishness. Calvin said he already felt Jewish before the trip, because he had taken on so much of the Jewish lifestyle including adopting a kosher diet and observing the discipline of Jewish prayer. Israel only enhanced the feeling because of the total immersion. I knew exactly how he felt.

Every place we visited and every activity we did in Israel was so deeply spiritual that it only fortified the concentrated studying we had been doing to prepare to be Jews. Encouraged by all the fine people we had met and befriended in Israel and at home along the way, at last, we felt prepared to face the Beis Din for our first meeting.

CHAPTER 18

THE PROCESS

Some people think Torah Judaism is merely a list of do's and don'ts which dictate what we eat, whom we can marry, when we should work, and what may and may not be done on the holidays we celebrate. Though it is true that Judaism does speak to these elements, the essence of Judaism, and what it offers to the world, is something much more profound. Judaism teaches us that we exist, constantly, in the presence of G-d, Who just over 3,300 years ago gave the Jewish people a set of instructions through Moses to guide humanity generally, and the Jewish people specifically, to living the most meaningful and rewarding life possible. It is not just a list of rules, but instead an attitude towards life.

Torah Judaism is a tremendous blessing as well as an awesome responsibility. That is why converting to Judaism is not a simple matter. Conversion requires a complete change of lifestyle and outlook. Since every aspect of a Torah Jew's life is governed by the Torah, a candidate must be ready to make a total commitment to changing his or her lifestyle by complete observance of Jewish law. This involves studying, accepting, and performing all of the mitzvos of the Torah as taught by the Sages of Israel throughout the centuries, and an unyielding commitment to moral and ethical behavior. The decision to convert cannot be made without extensive thought, prayer, learning, and preparation.

Rabbi Kaltmann scheduled our first interview with the Council of Orthodox Rabbis of Greater Detroit Beis Din, located in suburban Southfield, Michigan, in August 2011. The Beis Din is a rabbinical court that oversees kosher certifications, mikveh construction, Jewish divorces, conversions to Judaism, and other legal exchanges. In conversion cases, the responsibility of the Beis Din is to ascertain when candidates possess a sufficient amount of knowledge in and commitment to observing all of the laws and precepts of Judaism, that he or she is comfortable with the Jewish way of life, and is fully integrated into the Jewish community. We would need their permission to pursue conversion, and they would be the sole determinants of if and when we are ready to complete the conversion.

The members of the Beis Din would be familiar with our background, after having spoken with Rabbi Kaltmann and reviewing the paperwork describing our interest in Judaism. We knew that how we presented ourselves in this interview would determine whether we would be accepted, generating an excess of apprehension. The four-hour drive from Columbus to Southfield gave us plenty of time to work ourselves into a moderate state of anxiety; and since just Calvin and I were required at the initial meeting, we didn't have Rabbi Kaltmann to draw on for reassurance. The car ride was filled with alternating conjecture about what we might be asked, and quiet introspection. Despite the nervousness, we were both excited, too, to be taking this huge first step to making Judaism real for us.

We arrived fifteen minutes before our scheduled appointment, and were promptly greeted by one of the rabbis who told us to take a seat in the waiting area. More time to fret. Thankfully, only a few minutes later, it was time to meet the rabbis. We were ushered into an impressive meeting room containing a large conference table. Four esteemed rabbis occupied the chairs on one side of the table, leaving the opposing chairs for us. It was intimidating to sit facing these stoic authorities, knowing we would have to justify our desire and commitment to pursuing a halachic conversion to their satisfaction. Rabbi Neustadt, Rabbi Silberberg, Rabbi Bergstein, and Rabbi Kostelitz were imposing figures, but they all demonstrated kindness and fairness from the moment we started talking.

Because of the potential consequences to converts and to the Jewish people, initial questioning is focused on our motivation and the consideration we have given to the impact of converting. Fundamentally, the Beis Din must root out any ill-intended gentile who might be pursuing conversion only to promote Christianity in Israel or elsewhere. Furthermore, they are obliged to ensure that a convert, who will forever be a Jew, will be happy and observant post-conversion. The gravity of the objectives was not lost on us.

The rabbis had knowledge of our history as youth pastors in the church, which may have been a red flag to them regarding our intentions. They probably had not seen many legitimate converts who, after being wholly involved in a Christian church, had made such an about-face in their religious beliefs. We addressed their many questions concerning our change of heart from Christianity to Judaism to convince them we were completely detached from our earlier beliefs.

One technique the Beis Din uses to determine the level of commitment of a prospective convert is to point out that converting would make him part of a persecuted people. In fact, the Talmud states the first question the Beis Din should ask of any potential convert centers on this point. When we were asked, "Why do you want to be Jewish? Don't you know we're a persecuted people?", Calvin, unfazed, responded, "Brother, I'm black!" indicating he is well aware of what it means to be persecuted. Prejudice, mistreatment and exclusion were things we, Calvin in particular, had encountered before, and we assured the rabbis we could withstand any negativity we might encounter as Jews.

The rabbis emphasized that being a Jew is not an easy life, and they tried to dissuade us from converting no less than three times during that interview and at every subsequent meeting. They have the enormous responsibility of evaluating the seriousness of candidates, and whether or not they possess the fortitude to face the obstacles and challenges that will undoubtedly occur, including the impact on family and relationships. They also must judge the probability of a candidate's success in staying the course for a lifetime. They underscored again and again that we must be willing to adopt a total Orthodox lifestyle.

The bar is set very high to exclude all but the few who are willing and able to accept the demands of a halachic life. But they didn't know who they were dealing with. Calvin and I had already spent nearly 10 years poring over every morsel of religious instruction we could find and had already begun practicing many of the Jewish laws. We do not take our religion lightly and are not people who do things halfway – we wouldn't have been at this meeting if we weren't absolutely sure we were all in. And we offered every piece of evidence we could to prove our resolve.

We were asked to further verify our suitability by presenting the knowledge we had acquired regarding halacha, Jewish holidays, kashrus, and Shabbos. The years of Jewish studying we had done on our own, combined with the classes we attended at the Lori Schottenstein Chabad Center, seemed to satisfy the rabbis with our level of knowledge to that point.

Through most of the meeting, the rabbis challenged our position, but they also provided considerable consultation. We viewed this positively, because we figured the rabbis wouldn't take the time to advise if they weren't feeling pretty confident in our fitness for conversion. They explained the pitfalls that could happen along the way, citing that we still had two children living at home, giving them serious concern regarding how we would manage keeping kosher with non-Jews in the house, not to mention dealing with the feelings of those very non-Jews. We did not have a ready response to the kosher concerns, but Rabbi Bergstein came to our rescue with a practical solution to set up a non-kosher kitchen area in the basement with separate dishes and appliances. That would allow the kids to avoid the obstructions of a kosher kitchen while allowing us to maintain a strictly kosher kitchen.

By the end of the meeting, the rabbis were finally satisfied with our sincerity, and accepted us as candidates for conversion! We would need to move into a Jewish community, attend an Orthodox shul, and advance our knowledge through study and immersion in the lifestyle. They laid out the formal steps – acceptance of the mitzvos, *bris milah* (circumcision), and culminating with immersion in the mikveh – that would take one to two years to complete. Rabbi Bergstein told us, "This is a marathon, not a race. Enjoy it!" We left with instructions to continue studying and to come back in three months.

Despite all the help we had preparing for our meetings with the Beis

Din, we never knew what to expect. It was like walking into an exam without knowing the subject. They could pose obscure or obvious questions on topics ranging from Torah passages to High Holiday rituals to food handling, to prayers and blessings. I felt like we had to know everything, and tried to prepare for just that.

On our second visit with the Beis Din about four months later, Rabbi Kaltmann accompanied us. I crowded into the back seat of the car with the Shulchan Aruch, kosher kitchen books, Hebrew resources, Shabbos observance books, and resources on the brachos, so I could use the long drive as a final cram session. I read passages to Calvin while he drove to make sure we were both fresh. When we took our places across the table from the rabbis, Rabbi Kaltmann said, "Ask them anything. They know the answers!"

This second meeting with the Beis Din was just as intimidating as the first, at least for me. Again, we were quizzed at length and reminded of the magnitude of what we were doing. The rabbis attempted to deter us from going forward by telling us how long and bumpy the road would be. We reaffirmed our pledge to continue learning, and talked about the major challenge of physically moving into a Jewish community. The rabbis know that to fully understand what it will be like to live as a Torah Jew, living among other Torah Jews within an observant community is essential.

Although Calvin and I had known we would eventually have to leave our home and move into a Jewish community in order to convert, it was at the first Beis Din meeting that it became a directive. For our conversion to progress, we would need to be living amongst Orthodox Jews to ensure we could assimilate, to allow us to learn through daily observation, and to increase our halacha observance. We loved Chabad, and earnestly wanted to continue within that community, but we faced a number of obstacles, not the least of which was the proximity of the shul to affordable housing. The closest option we could find would entail a nearly two-mile walk each way on a busy road with no sidewalks to attend Shabbos services. It just wasn't practical. So the Beis Din pointed us to Congregation Ahavas Sholom, which is situated in the midst of a lovely Jewish neighborhood on the east side of Columbus, with ample housing.

We returned to Columbus feeling very excited and encouraged, but realizing we still had quite a road ahead of us. We immediately began to formulate our moving plan. It was going to take a good deal of money and elbow grease to get the home we had lived in for 14 years ready for market, and we wanted to give Hannah and Isaiah time to get used to the idea of being uprooted from the neighborhood where they had spent most of their lives.

Hannah was then a senior in high school and a move would require her to drive across town to get to school every day. Her friends all lived near or in our present neighborhood, and this meant not living down the street anymore from many of her friends. Isaiah was a freshman in college, and the move across town actually benefitted him as far as driving to campus; but most of his friends were in our old neighborhood where he would have preferred to stay. However, we had been discussing for a few years the idea of downsizing, and so they were not altogether surprised by the announcement.

Calvin and I came to realize that a family of eight who spends 14 years in one house accumulates A LOT of stuff! We knew we would be moving into a house no more than half the size of our current house, so the purge began. We told our kids who had left home already to reclaim any of their belongings they still wanted, and sold, gave away, or threw away loads of furniture, clothes, toys, sports equipment, and other junk. Nothing about this was easy or pleasant. I was prepared and motivated to just get rid of everything, but the sentimentality of my family members made for some hard bargaining about what to keep and what to liquidate. And, occasionally, I would have to part with something that was meaningful to me because it just wouldn't fit in our new life. In the end, it took about nine months to paint the walls, clean the carpets, repair broken things, clean up the landscaping, downsize our belongings, and get the house on the market.

In the meantime, we'd been looking for a home near the shul the Beis Din told us to attend. Incredibly, the second home we toured was the one that felt like home. It was a cozy, three-bedroom ranch that was so different from our spacious, six-bedroom two-story. It was quite an adjustment coming from a large house where we could go sometimes a whole day only seeing each other at dinner to a home where everything is on one level, yielding to more frequent interaction.

Leaving our old neighborhood also meant leaving Chabad. Rabbi Kaltmann of the Chabad shul was sad to see us go, and we were sad to go. After all, this was our first and only rabbi up to this point. We had friends there. It was very hard to leave, but we had already embraced so much change and were so utterly focused on our end goal that we said goodbye and forged ahead.

Our new home was a mere seven-tenths of a mile from Ahavas Sholom, and on the first Shabbos after moving in, we walked to the shul. As we walked up the street, toward our new shul, we felt like we were taking giant strides toward our goal of becoming Jews. It was somehow freeing to be able to abide by G-d's laws in one more way by not driving on Shabbos. In many ways, our feelings during that walk mirrored the ones we had when entering Chabad for that first Shabbos. We had the same apprehension about going to a shul where we didn't know any of the people, we didn't know their siddur, and we didn't know their routine. But this time, the trepidation was amplified by the fact that this was to be our permanent shul. It was even more important that we feel welcomed and that we fit in with this community. If things didn't gel for any reason, we would have no other option now that we had packed up our lives and settled into this community.

Once in the shul, Calvin and I parted, and I made my way to the women's seating area. Being new, I just wanted to slip in and get the lay of the land without drawing too much attention. There were many available seats, and I sat down in one near the middle of the women's section. A moment later a woman approached me and politely told me I was sitting in her seat. When I apologized and quickly moved a couple of seats over, the woman informed me that I was now in her daughter's seat. I stood up and felt like everyone's eyes were on me. I was self-conscious, even though no one was really paying me any mind. Shelley, a congregant who would soon become a good friend, sensing my discomfort, came right over to ask me to sit next to her. I went from feeling like an outsider to feeling welcomed within a moment's passing. Shelley helped me to navigate the siddur and patiently answered my questions about the service; and when I told her we were in the process of converting and had just moved into the community, she invited us over for a Shabbos meal. Through Shelley and her husband, Jack, we were introduced to other observant families who also extended meal invitations and took us into their fold. I think the people we met could discern our honest commitment and devotion to Judaism, leading to a whirlwind of introductions, inclusion and support.

I later learned it was the *yahrzeit* (anniversary of death) of the father of the woman whose seat I had taken. In Jewish tradition, when one loses a parent or other close relative, he or she moves to a different seat in the shul for one year. After the one-year mourning period, the deceased is remembered annually on their yahrzeit. She was not intentionally insensitive to me that first day in the shul. Her mind was obviously full with her own situation and she was not aware of mine. The woman phoned me later to explain the situation and to make amends. It was a minor slight that I felt was more due to my insecurity than to anything she had done, so I was more than willing to excuse the incident. This served as one of the many lessons in etiquette I learned through interacting with the Jewish community. Now I know it is considerate to ask those sitting near whether a certain seat is taken.

Once we met Rabbi Chaim Yosef Ackerman, the rabbi at Ahavas Sholom, we knew we had found our place. He would become our rock of support, both before and after our conversion. Initially, he and his wife, Menucha, invited us for Shabbos meals and even further extended our circle of role models by introducing us to more families. Later, when my mother was in intensive care following a stroke, Rabbi Ackerman drove 145 miles through a severe snow storm to visit and pray for her. The roads were so hazardous that it was impossible for him to drive home that night, and he stayed in a hotel before heading back to Columbus the next day. This meant so much to Yosef and me, and to my mother.

Not only were Calvin and I welcomed, but people went out of their way to include Hannah and Isaiah. Hannah became a highly sought-after babysitter for members of the shul. When we were invited for Shabbos meals, people would always tell us to bring them along. Our family had gone through a lot of changes, and Hannah and Isaiah had sacrificed for our choices. It was important to us that they not feel alienated because they are non-Jews living in a Jewish home and Jewish community. To our great delight, our children have participated with us in meals, Purim parties, and other social events at the shul. The community made sure that our children did not feel left out.

I have read and heard stories from other converts about being treated like second-class citizens, and that many born Jews have trouble accepting the convert as a legitimate Jew. Hashem gives 36 commandments in the Torah concerning proper treatment of converts, and He instructs Jews to remember the alienation they felt when they were strangers in Egypt. It is obvious in the way we were treated that the community where we reside takes this seriously, as they went out of their way to embrace us and extended their acceptance to us and our children.

When we were at Chabad, we were surrounded by mostly non-observant families, which was somewhat limiting to our growth. In contrast, enveloping ourselves in a Torah-observant community like Ahavas Sholom was the best way to absorb the realities of day-to-day Jewish living. We now can appreciate the Beis Din's wisdom in requiring us to live within the Jewish community. It is crucial that you are nurtured in a supportive environment and have observant people to emulate. Here you learn the ropes. It's one thing to read halacha from a book, but it's quite another when you watch observant families, see first-hand how they set up and run their kitchens, and witness how they observe Shabbos, and how they live. There's no substitute for this real-life experience. Practice makes perfect, and so we practiced with full hearts. We learned so much, and continue to do so. Another one of the beauties of Judaism: no matter how long you have been Jewish, and no matter how much you have learned, you are always learning.

About a year into our conversion, things were progressing nicely. We were living within the Jewish community, surrounding ourselves with

Torah observers, and continuing to develop our understanding of the faith. Rabbi Kaltmann was still our sponsor, but we were obviously having less interaction with him and more with Rabbi Ackerman. Rabbi Kaltmann spoke with Rabbi Ackerman about assisting with finishing up our conversion. We subsequently met with Rabbi Ackerman to formally request his sponsorship for the remainder of the process, since we were now under his care and observation. He had never been involved in a conversion, but agreed, since we were so far along.

Rabbi Ackerman went with us for our next visit to the Beis Din. The rabbis were very happy that we were now living in the Jewish community and walking to shul on Shabbos. Rabbi Ackerman confirmed that Calvin was davening with a *minyan* (quorum of ten men over the age of 13 required for traditional Jewish public worship) three times every day. The rabbis were especially impressed with our submission of the outlines Yerachmiel created for our studies with him, and with the certificates for the three-month courses I had taken in Kosher Kitchen and Shabbos Kitchen. These items were above and beyond what was prescribed by the Beis Din, and further demonstrated our dedication to the process. This visit really added to our confidence.

We traveled to the Southfield Beis Din one more time, for the final approval process, before being scheduled for the mikveh. Our daughter Hannah always saw how nervous I was about these visits to the Beis Din. She was such a cheerleader for us during the process, and this message she left for me to find on my iPad later was exactly what we needed to hear.

January 12, 2013

Dear Mom and Dad,

I love you guys so much and I hope you have a good time in Detroit tomorrow. I know you're nervous, but you'll do fine. You and Dad are very dedicated and I'm very proud of what you've learned and the strong relationship you guys have with G-d. I can only hope that one day my relationship and trust in G-d is as strong as yours. Please don't be worried about this meeting, because from what I've seen, you seem ready. I'll be praying for you. You are amazing parents. I love you.

Hannah

After one house move, two shuls, two sponsors, five visits to the Beis Din; after 2,110 miles, and 40 hours in the car; after hundreds of hours of classes and tutoring; after thousands of pages of reading; and after 19 months – the goal line was in sight. The Beis Din gave us their approval to schedule the mikveh, the immersion ritual that is the capstone of the conversion process, the birth of our Jewish selves.

CHAPTER 19

THE BIG DAY

The momentous day of our conversion, for which we had intensely prepared, had finally arrived. February 28, 2013 was the day we would formally say goodbye to our non-Jewish identities and assume our Jewish selves. Overcome with a flurry of emotions, from anticipation and anxiety to accomplishment and serenity, we once again pointed our car north to see the Beis Din rabbis.

Our destination this time was West Bloomfield Township, Michigan, not far from the Beis Din headquarters in Southfield. We headed to Rabbi Silberberg's shul, Bais Chabad Torah Center, where a mikveh was located, for the culmination of our hard work, study, relocation, and many emotional ups and downs.

The night before the conversion, Yosef recalls feeling a sense of panic thinking about the awesome responsibility that would soon be part of his life. He realized the seriousness of this final step and knew that after immersion, there was no turning back. But he also realized this was what his soul had been yearning for, and he was confident that Hashem had brought him this far and would not abandon him on his journey.

I had elected not to tell my mother about the conversion until just a few months before the conversion ceremony. I was afraid she would react negatively, and I wanted to avoid any distraction to the deeply affirmative reverence I had maintained throughout the progression of finding truth. When I ultimately mustered the courage to tell her, it turned out my fears were unwarranted. She was not all that surprised, because she was aware of our studying and involvement with Judaism for several years. She was curious and genuinely interested in the process. On my next trip to Toledo I gave her some books to read about conversion. She called me one day to say she had "hundreds of questions." She had read every book I gave her and kept a notebook of her queries. We went through her myriad questions, one by one, until she was satisfied with my explanations. She then expressly requested to attend the ceremony in Michigan.

I was so blessed to have the two most important women in my life – my mother and my precious daughter Hannah – not only support our decision to convert, but to personally attend the conversion ceremony with us. It brings tears to my eyes when I think about how loved and strengthened I felt when making this enormous transition. I hold this memory dear in my heart, and hope they both know how much their support meant to me.

Hashem brought precisely the people we needed to help us along in the process of conversion, and several were there to witness the conversion. Yerachmiel and Chayala, who had invested in us so heavily during the conversion preparation process, Rabbi Ackerman, our sponsor, and his wife, Menucha, who served as my *shomeret* (mikveh attendant), and my best friend, April, were there to see us begin our new lives as part of the Jewish people. When we came out of the mikveh, they told us how proud they were and happy that we could finally reap our reward after all the years of work and sacrifice. And, I believe, they found it personally gratifying to be instruments in bringing two new Jews into the fold.

Once at the shul, Calvin and I went our separate ways for our respective activities. The next time we would lay eyes on each other, we would be Jews. I went into the preparation room while our friends and family waited in another room. Immersion in the mikveh actualizes the transition between the convert's old identity and new one as a Jew. To ensure there is no barrier between my body and the water, I had to follow specific preparations. I bathed for 45 minutes, then showered to rinse clean. Menucha, as my attendant, is responsible for confirming I have adequately prepared myself and, at the time of immersion, that all parts of my body and hair are fully submerged.

While I was readying myself, Calvin was with the three Beis Din rabbis – Rabbi Silberberg, Rabbi Neustadt, and Rabbi Bergstein – and the *mohel* (ritual circumciser), to complete his required circumcision and mikveh blessing. He had been circumcised at birth, but medical circumcision does not fulfill the conversion requirement. In order to forge his Covenant with G-d, a *hatafat dam brit* (ritual extraction of a drop of blood) is performed. Calvin is no different from most grown men in that the procedure feels highly personal and invasive. Despite the minor physical and not-so-minor psychological discomfort of the procedure, he approached it with the earnest understanding of its importance. He also confirms what other converts had told him – the importance outweighs any pain, and the anticipation was worse than the actual event.

Leading up to the mikveh, Calvin was asked several times if he was sure he wanted to proceed. There is no shortage of opportunity to back out of the decision. He confirmed each time he was asked that, yes, he was sure he wanted to be a Jew. When he was standing in the water, the rabbis asked him to confirm that he understood the finality of his action, and that when he completed his immersion, he would be a full-fledged Jew, with all the attendant responsibilities that carries. He confirmed again with a full heart. He recited the blessing, dunked fully underwater, and emerged a Jew.

I know Calvin was nervous leading up to his conversion, primarily because of the dreaded pinprick, and I was nervous about baring my body for the immersion. I understood the symbolism and the sanctity of the ritual, and I also appreciated that everyone else in the room respected that sanctity. However, being naked, draped in only a sheet, in a room with other people, especially the rabbis, was a distraction impossible to shake. I did all I could to put aside my self-consciousness, focus on the sacredness of the act, and embrace the experience. I wish I had been more successful in letting go of the vulnerability I felt, because I know I would have enjoyed it more.

Once I was standing on the steps of the mikveh, draped in the sheet, my back to the rabbis, I was filled with an inner calm, cohabitating with my hyperawareness of the rabbis' presence. My mom, Hannah, Chayala and April were standing just outside the room, but were able to see and hear what was happening. I, too, was given several opportunities to back out. One rabbi said, "It's not too late to change your mind." I reaffirmed my resolve and walked into the water. The rabbis asked a string of questions to make sure that I grasped the seriousness of accepting and observing the Torah, forever. I was reminded that my decision would be permanent and irrevocable. After what felt like an eternity but was likely just a few moments, it was time to say the bracha and immerse. Menucha tenderly adjusted my sheet, thoughtfully protecting my dignity, and explaining how I would allow the sheet to hover in the water around me, without touching me. Her care added to my sense of calm. This was the moment we had been preparing for, and longing for. I said the blessing, and immersed. And then – it was over, just like that. I emerged from the mikveh as a Jew!

After the mikveh, we gathered with our friends, family, and rabbis in the social hall of the shul for refreshments. Apparently, my mom still had some lingering questions about conversion to Judaism, so she had a long conversation with Rabbi Bergstein. He commented later that she was delightful, and it was obvious to him that she was sincerely supportive of our decision and fascinated by the process. When asked what stood out the most about that day, Yerachmiel told me he remembered my mom and her interest in what was happening. She made quite an impression on those who were there.

Calvin and I felt a sense of relief and exhilaration. We had finally reached our goal, after many years and much study. However, this emotional high was also tempered by the sobering knowledge that we were now totally responsible for all the mitzvot as if we were born Jews.

The rabbis then gave us their blessings, and also officially introduced us with our Hebrew names. Sometimes the rabbis will assign names to converts, but we had previously chosen names and the rabbis approved. We were no longer Calvin and Jeri, but now Yosef and Emunah.

I chose the Hebrew name of Emunah Vered. The English meaning of Emunah is "faith" or "faithfulness to G-d." I felt like it was so relevant and characterized my life. I chose the middle name Vered, which means Rose, in honor of my maternal grandmother, who was so inexplicably drawn to Judaism. Calvin chose the Hebrew name Yosef because he always loved the stories of Yosef in the Bible, and thought of him as an excellent role model. Yosef means, "G-d will increase."

On our drive back to Columbus, we reflected on whether we felt different after our conversion, and realized we really did not. It was anticlimactic after looking forward to this for almost two years. We expected more of a revelation. But we had already been living as Jews, were very much connected to the Jewish community and our shul, and most of the transformation in our lives had already occurred. Our day-to-day life was virtually the same as it had been the previous day, just with new names.

Rabbi Ackerman reflected on the day as "powerful and profound in an intangible way." Joyful events are usually filled with singing and dancing, and ours was more private and personal, which he felt made it special in a deep way. We were so appreciative of his willingness to take on our conversion midstream and with such a busy schedule, but we think he was equally appreciative of being able to participate in the moment.

The Columbus Jewish Community was a key factor in our successful conversion. We had been welcomed immediately and warmly received at Shabbos and Yom Tov meals. We never felt alone or were treated as outsiders. I hate to think what would have happened had we not had this tremendous support system. I don't think our fellow Jews realize just how much their non-judgmental attitude and willingness to patiently tutor us during the learning process made things so much easier. I feel like we were gently and lovingly taught and nurtured, and this loving, nurturing teaching continues to this day.

It can make the difference between people sticking with their conversion or walking away from Judaism altogether. When I recite the passage for the welfare of the converts in the daily prayers, it is a daily reminder of how much Hashem loves us. It is humbling to realize that Hashem foresaw people like us, converts of later generations who would decide to commit their lives to the Jewish destiny, and made sure we would be treated with love and respect by specific commandments in the Torah regarding converts.

There are similarities between Abraham, who was commanded, *"Lech Lecha,"* (often translated as "go for yourself," or "go to yourself") and the journey of a convert. Converts must leave their familiar life, their home, and go to a new, unfamiliar place. They are on a very lonely path as far as lacking Jewish family traditions, growing up without Hebrew, not knowing familiar holiday songs; and Jewish community support is a critical aspect in the entire process of feeling loved and accepted. Our open-mindedness and desired intimacy with Hashem brought us this immense reward. Converts are Abraham's and Sarah's children; and just like Abraham and Sarah, converts have to be daring and unafraid of what people think to withstand the pressure.

Of course, building a Jewish identity takes time. We sometimes feel lost, because we don't have the cultural upbringing, family traditions passed down to us, or the benefit of attending Hebrew school in our youth. We keep reminding ourselves that our new Jewish identities will take time to develop, and we must keep pushing forward. This illustrates the absolute importance of living in a community and being surrounded by people who are willing to take the time to nurture you. A convert has to find his way, within the bounds of halacha of course, to a form of Judaism that speaks to him. We understand how some converts can become disillusioned. Born Jews are not necessarily always on a search for truth. They accept Judaism because that is what they were taught. They may believe it, but the question of authenticity is not necessarily a priority for them. This, of course, is a very unique experience for most converts, and most certainly was for us.

Two days after the conversion, we celebrated our first Shabbos as Jews. This was the first time we would be able to observe in totality. Because non-Jews are not able to observe all mitzvot, we had always ended the day with a flip of a light switch or some other action that would "break" Shabbos. As Jews, we now had to observe in totality, but more importantly to us, we were ABLE to observe in totality. We were grateful for the privilege.

The parasha for the week of our conversion was *Ki Tisa* (translated as "when you take"). This was meaningful to us in that it contains the reminder for the Children of Israel to keep the Sabbath, and that it is an everlasting covenant between G-d and the Children of Israel. We became even more aware after our conversion that Shabbos was going to be the anchor of the entire week. When we were initially exposed to Judaism, Shabbos was what really had an impact on us – such a beautiful and profound gift from Hashem to His people. We honestly don't know how we ever lived without it.

Also in this parasha, Moses inscribes the covenant on the second set of Tablets – a covenant of which we were now a part. What an awesome privilege and responsibility! The *Haftorah* (a selection from one of the biblical books of the prophets) for that week was the incident of Elijah and the prophets of Baal, when the people who witnessed this spectacle finally came to the realization that G-d is the only Ultimate Power in the world. What a meaningful Torah and Haftorah for the week of our conversion!

While we didn't have the tremendous revelation we thought we might directly following our conversion, we did each have moments where it became real to us. Yosef received his first official aliyah on that first Shabbos. Aliyah means ascent or going up, and is the honor of standing at the *bimah* (raised platform in the synagogue from which the Torah is read) to recite the blessings over the Torah. Aliyah in this sense refers to the physical ascent of the person to the bimah and the spiritual uplifting associated with participation in this hallowed ritual. I was filled with so much pride, and the tears just came. Five years later, I still feel the same way every time he gets called up to the Torah. My heart swells every time I hear him being called up for an aliyah, "Yosef ben Avraham," which means son of Avraham, since all male converts take the patriarch Avraham as their spiritual father. Likewise, female converts take the matriarch Sarah as their spiritual mother.

My moment of realism came the following Monday when I donned a *sheitel* (Yiddish for wig) for the first time to go to work. I wanted to avoid any potential negative consequences, so had only told my boss about the conversion. I worried that when I walked in with a sheitel that it would be obvious to everyone in the office and would draw awkward questions. But no questions and no strange looks came my way. If anyone did notice, they just took it in stride and went about their business. I was relieved and thankful that

I live and work where personal choices are accepted.

We may not have felt a monumental transformation at the moment of conversion because of our extensive preparation, but it did finally set in and we *were* different. We were truly a part of something. In the backs of our minds, we kept returning to the fact that we were actually Jews, handling the thought as if it were a beautiful gem. We turned it over and over, getting used to the smooth facets and sharp edges. There had been so much preparation and planning for this moment that passed so quickly. It would just take some time until saying "I am Jewish" would not feel foreign but indeed natural.

CHAPTER 20

UNDER THE CHUPPAH

The days following the *geirus* (conversion) were a whirlwind of activity. According to Jewish law, our Christian marriage was not considered legitimate, which meant Yosef and I could not live in the same house after the conversion. When we returned to Columbus, I came to our house to sleep and Yosef went to stay at a friend's home until we could be officially wed under the *chuppah* (wedding canopy), which was to take place three days later, on Sunday.

My friend, Elaine, sponsored a *Shabbos Kallah* (a gathering of women to offer blessings and good tidings to the bride, on the Shabbos before the wedding). The Shabbos Kallah is structured as an open house, and all women in the Jewish community are welcome to attend. Many women from the shul attended, as well as my mother and daughter. It was special for me to have them there with me, in a way bridging my old and new identities.

Several of the women who offered blessings spoke about how Yosef and I had been an inspiration to the community, because we are so passionate and proud to be Jews. I think our passion reminds those lifelong Jews, whose enthusiasm with the awesomeness of Judaism may have waned, to rejoice in their beliefs and observances. I had seen my mom weather setbacks and tragedy with dry eyes, but while someone was talking I glanced over to see a tear slipping down her cheek. She was so touched by what people had to say. It was a beautiful gathering, and I will forever treasure the memories.

On Sunday, Yosef and I woke up in separate dwellings, but we would be reunited after we pledged ourselves to G-d and each other under Jewish law at our chuppah. The marriage canopy is raised over the heads of the *chosson* and *kallah* (bride and groom) as a symbol of the Jewish home that will be built and shared by the couple. It is open on all sides, just as Abraham and Sarah had their tent open on all sides to welcome people with warm and generous hospitality.

It was important to me that our non-Jewish family in attendance would be able to understand what was happening; so I created cards that outlined the rituals and traditions, and placed them on the seats in the sanctuary for reference.

This event was truly a community effort, with many people helping to make the day a beautiful *simcha* (Jewish celebration). I arrived at the shul to find many men and women buzzing about, making preparations. Men were setting up the chuppah, and women were preparing salads and arranging trays of food. It was all a bit chaotic until Chayala, who is a wedding and event planner, began giving directions for a more coordinated approach. She had also surprised me by bringing the centerpieces for all the tables.

While I was overseeing activities in the kitchen, Yosef was seated at a table with Rabbi Ackerman, receiving information about his obligations according to the *kesubah* (marriage contract). The kesubah is an important document in traditional Jewish marriages that sets forth the chosson's rights and responsibilities related to the kallah.

As with most weddings, there were things that didn't quite go as expected and last-minute changes we had to make. Our photographer told us a few days prior to the wedding of an unavoidable schedule conflict, leading to a scramble for a replacement. Our friend, Bob donated his DJ equipment and planned to act as DJ, but also had another obligation. Another friend, Avi, easily stepped in as the DJ. In spite of the few hiccups, and thanks to our friends and family, it was a perfectly beautiful day.

The men's side of the sanctuary was filled to capacity, with people standing in the back. There were friends from four or five different shuls, family members, and many distinguished rabbis in attendance. Yosef donned his *kittel* (a white robe which symbolizes purity, worn on special occasions by Jewish men, such as at the Passover Seder and on Yom Kippur, and by the bridegroom when he is getting married). Traditionally, the bride's mother walks the bride down the aisle and around the groom under the chuppah; but because my mom is not Jewish I needed to have someone else do the honor. My rebbetzin, Menucha Ackerman, granted my request to be my escort.

As Rebbetzin Ackerman walked me down the aisle, our friend Yerachmiel sang a beautiful song. We ascended the steps to the chuppah, and Rebbetzin Ackerman ushered me around Yosef seven times. There are seven wedding blessings given to the kallah and chosson under the chuppah. We had the highest honor of having distinguished rabbis and dear friends bestow these blessings upon us.

In addition to the cards I had provided, Rabbi Ackerman did a thorough job of explaining everything as the ceremony proceeded. This was important, because our non-Jewish family and friends were there to support us, including my mom, children, my brother, Carey, three sisters, Lori, Elisa and Erin, as well as nieces, a cousin, and an aunt, and we wanted them to understand the meaning of the different rituals, as they had never attended a Jewish wedding. Rabbi Ackerman also gave a meaningful talk about Yosef and me.

Almost all Jewish weddings, religious or secular, conclude with the stomping on and breaking of a glass by the chosson. This ritual has been interpreted to signify the breaking or cutting of something to seal a covenant (marriage), the end of the tranquility of the ceremony, and most solemnly, the destruction of the Temple in Jerusalem. The loud noise of breaking glass is meant to sober revelers and remind them that even at the height of rejoicing, we should recall the pain and losses suffered by the Jewish people. While still under the chuppah, a napkin-wrapped glass was placed on the floor in front of Yosef's foot. He brought his foot firmly down, and with a pop, the glass was shattered. Cries of "Mazel Tov!" filled the air.

Yosef and I walked arm-in-arm down the aisle, through the crowds of people who were clapping and shouting. We then went into the *yichud* (seclusion) room (Rabbi Ackerman's office). According to normal Jewish custom, the bride and groom have never been alone together, having only been in public places throughout the courtship, and have not seen each other at all for the week leading up to the wedding. The couple is brought to a private room where they can talk privately and break the fast customary before the ceremony. Someone is posted outside the room to ensure that the couple is not interrupted. These moments of seclusion signify their new status of living together as husband and wife. Yosef and I were too overwhelmed to say much, even at this most private of moments. This moment seemed surreal, and we could not believe that the magical day had finally arrived, and that we had just experienced our second wedding, our chuppah!

While we were in seclusion, family and friends were busy preparing the social hall for dancing and the reception. There were several surprises awaiting Yosef. Bob had arranged for the Ohio State Buckeye Battle Cry song to be played as we came out to greet people. This was a great moment, and Yosef was absolutely delighted. After we entered the social hall together, we were individually steered to the separate men's and women's dancing areas. At an Orthodox wedding, there is a *mechitzah* (divider separating the two sections), and there was wild dancing on both sides! No Jewish wedding is complete without the famous chair dance. In this tradition, a few strong and brave guests hoist the bride and groom high above the crowd on chairs, surrounded by friends and family dancing in ecstatic circles, as the elevated couple tries not to look, or fall, down. Entertaining the bride and groom on their wedding day is not only a mitzvah, but also an obligation. At one point, our oldest son, Cal Jr., put his dad upon his shoulders and danced around with him.

After a long session of frenetic dancing, we took a break to eat the wonderful food that had been prepared. People took turns saying something about us or giving us a blessing, and we each addressed our friends and family. Lana had made a beautiful wedding cake, almost too beautiful to eat. She also surprised Yosef with cake lollipops in the shape of footballs to complement the OSU Buckeyes theme.

After months and months of planning and preparing, the day

came and went too quickly. It was surreal to think we were now, officially, Jewish man and wife.

CHAPTER 21

ISRAEL AS JEWS – 2014

The following year, Yosef and I would travel to Israel once again, this time as Jews. We again decided to go during Sukkot, because it is such a delightful time to be in Israel. I was curious: would it feel different to be in the magnificent Holy Land as Jews than it had on previous visits? Would we see the religious sites any differently than we had before? Would people treat us differently?

My early trips to Israel were either pre-planned sets of activities through the tour company, or my self-made itinerary including every religious site and tour possible. Every time I had gone to Israel, I had met someone new who would become a friend to see on subsequent trips. This made trying to fit in all the sightseeing and personal visits a bit of a juggling exercise when planning a new trip. It's a good problem to have.

This time we were going to spend the first two weeks of our three-week visit in Jerusalem so we could tour Rachel's Tomb, the Cave of Machpelah, Tel Shiloh, and to observe the *Birkat Kohanim* (Priestly blessing) at the Kotel. We would then go north to Tiveria and Tsfat where we were to meet some old and new friends. We planned to meet Rena, the woman Ahuvah had introduced to Yosef and me when we were in Israel a couple of years before, and Riva, Yerachmiel's daughter. It was always amazing to me how open the Jewish community is, as if there is no stranger among them.

Earlier in the year, I was listening to a show on Israel National News called "Aliyah Time." The hosts were interviewing a woman by the name of Rivkah Lambert Adler, who lives in Ma'ale Adumim, and specifically in the religious neighborhood of Mitzpeh Nevo. This was a locale Yishai Fleisher had mentioned to us during our radio interview in Israel in 2012, when he suggested we explore neighborhoods for aliyah purposes. I couldn't believe that she actually lived in the place he had told us about. Again, *Yad Hashem* (the hand, so to speak, of G-d)!

In the interview, Rivkah provided useful information about the religious makeup of the neighborhood, the number of English speakers, and services for new *olim* (people who make aliyah; Jewish immigrants to Israel). She spoke with such passion and love for the place where she lived that I found myself riveted to the program and, somehow, to her. I decided to send an email to express my enjoyment of her interview and ask her if she would be interested in meeting us when we came to Israel. She replied that she would be more than happy to give us a tour and answer any questions we had. I scheduled this side trip into our itinerary, and we kept in touch periodically via email for the months leading up to the trip.

I rented an apartment in Jerusalem that would serve as our home base between tours and sightseeing. It was a quaint dwelling with a beautiful garden, and was within walking distance of restaurants, shopping and bus stops. It was comforting to have a place to stay for a longer duration that didn't feel temporary.

One of our first tours was to Rachel's Tomb, and then to the city of Hevron. The tomb of the biblical matriarch, Rachel, is located at the northern entrance of Bethlehem, about 300 meters up the road from Jerusalem's Gilo neighborhood. Because of aggression towards Jews, the only safe way for us to access the site is to go through the tunnel underneath *Beit Lechem* (Bethlehem). When we came out on the other side, we were standing in a fortress complete with concrete walls and watchtowers. The building where the tomb is housed is reinforced with concrete barriers and more guard towers.

Since the time of her burial more than 3000 years ago, the Tomb of Rachel has always been a special place for prayer. Rachel ultimately came to be considered the mother of the Jewish people, and she is a symbol of hope for all those in need of special blessing. She teaches us the power of prayer. Rachel's Tomb is a living symbol of Hashem's promise to Rachel that her children will return to the Land of Israel. To pray at the tomb of *Rochel Imeinu* (Rachel our mother) was an incredible and emotional experience.

In Hevron, we had the privilege of viewing the Cave of Machpelah, the final resting place for Abraham, Sarah, Isaac, Rebekah, Jacob, and Leah. The building over the tomb, constructed by Herod the Great over 2000 years ago, is truly amazing in its dimensions and complexity.

I had been so moved by videos of the Birkat Kohanim at the Kotel that I have been watching them for years on YouTube, and I made sure we would be able to participate during our visit. This event takes place twice a year during the intermediate days of Sukkot and Pesach. An impressive number of *Kohanim* (descendants of the priestly tribe) join together in one voice to bless the Jewish nation. We left the apartment early, and joined the many thousands of people who were making their way into the Old City. What a powerful experience, to be blessed by such a great number of priests! I am so very grateful for the opportunity to receive this blessing, and to have experienced this event first-hand.

On another day we ventured to the Shomron (Samaria) to see Tel Shiloh, religiously significant to Jews for several reasons. Our friends, Bruce and Nancy from Columbus, suggested we meet his son and daughter-in-law, Yehuda and Adina, who live in Achiya, a community located in the Shomron. Yehuda gave us a thorough tour of Shiloh. Tel Shiloh is mentioned in the book of Joshua, as the tribe of Ephraim brought the Tabernacle here, making Shiloh a religious center even before Jerusalem. It is possible to stand at the exact place on Tel Shiloh where some scholars believe the Tabernacle stood. This is also the location where the biblical figure Hannah came to pray for a son. Later she dedicated that son, Samuel, to serve in the Tabernacle.

After the tour, we traveled up the mountain to their home where Adina made us a wonderful lunch. They live in a magnificent place, high atop a mountain, with spectacular views and a peacefulness like nowhere else. It was great to make two more friends in Israel and to see such a commanding biblical site.

When we had arrived in Israel, I contacted Rivkah to make arrangements for a visit to Ma'ale Adumim. She and her husband, Rabbi Elan Adler, invited us to their sukkah for a snack while we got acquainted. It was obvious that Rivkah and I cared deeply about many of the same things and felt a strong connection. Although Jewish from birth, her story echoes mine in many ways, resulting in a special kinship. She became religious as an adult and felt Hashem chose her to come to Israel, making aliyah after embracing Judaism. I also felt some familiarity with Rabbi Adler, because I had regularly listened to a radio show he hosted on Israel National Radio called the Derech Eretz Show.

After we ate, they gave us a tour of their apartment, and then took us out on their balcony, and explained the topography of the land. We then drove all over their neighborhood, Mitzpeh Nevo, looking at several different apartment styles, checking out the neighborhood market, and winding up at the mall, where we had lunch in the food court. As they showed us the sights, they explained what living in Israel was like after leaving the U.S. This time with them went a long way to helping us visualize making the move.

By now the aliyah idea had taken root, but only as something we would do in the future, after we retired. While the work I do can be done anywhere, Yosef's job is in Columbus, and we are still dependent on dual incomes. At this point we were thinking that after retirement, still ten years away, we would make plans to live in Israel part-time. Visiting Ma'ale Adumim was really a fact-gathering expedition to assist in future planning. At that point, it was nothing more.

Rivkah suggested we open a bank account to start depositing shekels for our future. She provided us with the name of a contact at the Bank of Jerusalem, gave us several books to read, e-mailed many helpful websites, and offered to help us in any way that we needed. What a wonderful connection! The Adlers even offered us their guest room for our next trip. Rivkah would end up being a real cheerleader for us in our hopes and dreams to make aliyah.

Yosef and I thought Rivkah's suggestion about opening a bank account was a good one and took advantage of her referral. This is how we became acquainted with Yonatan, and later we would meet his wife Bina. What an incredible blessing it was to meet him! He is a caring, spiritual, kind, and helpful person. He was happy to meet us, and helped us open a savings account. We were so excited to take this small step toward possibly living in Israel someday. Making small talk, we told him we were going to Ramat Beit Shemesh the last few days of our trip to visit with a friend's daughter. His eyes bright with delighted surprise, he told us that is where he lives. We left the bank, confident that we had had taken our first tangible step toward future aliyah, and had made yet another friend in Israel.

We rounded out our time in Jerusalem with a concert at the Jerusalem Theatre, conveniently on the same street as our apartment. One of my favorite Jewish musicians, Yaakov Shwekey, was performing at a fundraiser for United Hatzalah of Israel. It was a sold-out concert, and for good reason. He put on an outstanding show, singing some of my favorite songs such as "Cry No More," and "Vehi Sheamda." It made my heart sing to be there hearing these beautiful songs live. As we sat there enjoying the concert, Yosef felt a tap on his shoulder. He turned around and there sat Avi our friend from Columbus who had been the DJ at our wedding! The Jewish world is indeed small.

After spending two weeks in Jerusalem, we traveled north to Tiveria and then to Tsfat. We had visited Tsfat in 2012, but this time was different. Yosef was able to immerse himself in the Ari's Mikveh this time, since he was now a Jew. This mikveh was quite different than the one he'd been in for our conversion. Fed by an ice-cold underground stream, the mikveh's cavernous pool is cut from the stone, virtually in the side of the mountain. It's a hike to get there, roughly 100 steps either descending from the mountain top or climbing up from the base. The effort to get there is worth it, and physically embodies the effort Yosef exerted to spiritually and religiously be permitted to enjoy the beautiful experience. While he was in the mikveh, I stood outside overlooking the ancient cemetery, feeling a sense of joy and extreme gratitude for what we now had.

With only three days remaining in our trip, we traveled from the north back to Jerusalem, and then on to Ramat Beit Shemesh. There we were met by Yerachmiel's daughter, Riva, and shepherded to her family's apartment several blocks from the bus stop. Knowing Riva's father, it wasn't surprising to see this was a close family, with parents committed to each other and their children.

Yosef went to daven Kabbalat Shabbat at a shul across the street from where we were staying. Two incredible things happened here. First, he was able to be counted in the minyan, since he now was a Jew. While he had been davening for years by this time, being considered one of the minyan felt like it legitimized his participation. He felt closer to Hashem and recognized for what he was in his heart.

Second, Yosef ran into Yonatan, from the bank. Of course, he had told us he lived in the area, but in a city of 25,000, we didn't expect to see him. It turns out Yonatan lived only doors away from Riva's apartment. He invited us to come to his house to meet his wife, Bina, and we took him up on his offer. We were so delighted to have two *more* friends in Israel.

The next day, we had a delicious Shabbat lunch with our hosts. Riva is quite a cook, and what a treat it was to sit at her table! Motzei Shabbat, I had the good fortune of going to hear one of my favorite singers, Ari Goldwag. It turns out he lives in Ramat Beit Shemesh, and was doing a free concert at a neighborhood shul. Riva and her daughter, Penina, walked with me to the concert. It was so incredible to see him performing "Am Echad" live and in person. It was also a little sad in some ways, too, as the next morning we were to leave Beit Shemesh, and leave Israel.

All of my experiences from each trip built upon one another, further strengthening my connection to G-d and the land of Israel. Each time I left, I felt a deeper and deeper sadness upon leaving. You are on such a spiritual high when in Israel, and when you come back to the U.S., as much as you try to hold onto that higher level of spirituality, each day it slowly fades away. There is a special *kedusha* (holiness) about the land. Either on the plane ride home or upon arriving home, I would start planning the next trip. My mom would say, "Why don't you go somewhere different? You've already been there!" She just did not understand that it was as if part of my root system was there and I couldn't be fully nourished until I was back in that land. Sometimes words are just not adequate to express what is in your heart and soul.

After this trip, the desire to live in the land began to grow exponentially. When I came back to the U.S., I found myself thinking about making aliyah quite often. It seemed it was always on my mind; and I would frequently wonder how it would be to actually live in the land. I joined online forums, registered with Nefesh B'Nefesh (a nonprofit organization that promotes and facilitates aliyah), watched webinars, and spoke with other interested parties. I eventually started an aliyah support group, with monthly meetings at my house to share ideas, encourage one another, and discuss possible struggles and challenges in moving to a foreign country. My new motto became, "Dream it, Believe it, Plan it, Achieve it." Dreaming it – check; Believing it – check; Planning it – involves massive amounts of information-gathering, making connections, etc. My daily prayer was that Hashem would allow me the privilege and merit of someday making aliyah, and that I would be worthy to receive such a gift. Of course, I could never leave my kids and grandkids year-round. I thought maybe at some point in the future it would be possible to live in Israel part-time and the U.S. part-time, thus enabling me to have the best of both worlds: my family and Israel.

The answer to the question of whether it would feel different to be in Israel as a Jew, we discovered, is an emphatic yes. We no longer felt like we were on the outside looking in, but that we were bona fide members of the global Jewish community. Everything we felt on previous trips was enhanced by this feeling of contentment and gratitude that we had in our hearts. All of the people we have met and the relationships we have formed are expanding our reach into and fortifying our bond with the Jewish population. Yes, it feels different. It feels right.

CHAPTER 22

EPILOGUE

After my sixth trip to Israel as a tourist, my yearning for Israel only intensified. My husband and I had discussed living in Israel part-time after retirement, which at that point was seven years away. I thought to myself, "Please G-d, I want to go now. I want to make a difference NOW." By making aliyah and becoming an Israeli citizen, you have the opportunity to build a stronger Israel by such things as influencing Israeli policy, bolstering the economy and, if you are a young person, serving in the Israel Defense Forces. This idea bloomed, and after several months of contemplation, I approached Yosef with a plan. I suggested I would live in Israel part of the year, and in the U.S. part of the year. As it happened, Rabbi Lazer Brody was coming to Columbus to speak, and we scheduled a private meeting with him to discuss this idea. His advice was that if I had *parnassa* (a way to make a living), if Yosef and I were in agreement, and if Yosef and I would not be apart for any longer than 90 days at a stretch, he felt it was okay for me to make aliyah. Yosef was not ready at that point to make aliyah, as he was finishing a degree at The Ohio State University. He gave me his permission to make aliyah, get things set up and put down roots; he would join me when he completed his degree. We agreed on a one-year trial period, and if at the end of one year, we felt our marriage was suffering in any way, all bets were off, and I would return to Ohio. After getting his consent, I needed to move to the next stage, which was coming up with parnassa. I wanted to come to Israel debt-free, with enough money in the bank to sustain me for one year. With Hashem's help, and through a series of miraculous events, this materialized. All during this time, I recited my mantra every day: "Dream it, Believe it, Plan it, Achieve it."

Nine months after I first approached Yosef about this plan, I made aliyah on the Nefesh B'Nefesh charter flight, August 17, 2016. There were 233 olim, the youngest being three-and-a-half-weeks, and the eldest, 85 years. There were 75 young people who would be joining the Israel Defense Forces (IDF). The pilot made an announcement just before touchdown in Israel saying, "You may have landed in Israel many times before, but this time when you land you will be an Israeli citizen," at which point a wild cheer and singing broke out on the plane! Several friends came to the welcome ceremony at the airport including Barry and Adele from Netanya and Ruti and Avi from Neve Daniel.

We had made two pilot trips to Ma'ale Adumim; and that is where I landed, joining a beautiful, warm and welcoming community in the Judean Desert. Friends Yonatan and Bina from Ramat Beit Shemesh had gone over to the apartment prior to my arrival and decorated the door with signs and balloons to welcome me.

Several key people made sure I had a "soft landing" upon my arrival in Israel, assuring I had invites for Shabbat meals, helping me acclimate to life in an unfamiliar culture, making sure I was on the right bus, translating my mail, and a myriad of other day-to-day challenges. They have become dear friends and I am so very grateful for them. Rivkah and Elan, Chaya Bluma, Zahavah and Ovadia, and Tova. Even my first landlady and friend, Susan, made sure my refrigerator and cupboard were full of food when I arrived as well. There are many others in my very special neighborhood of Mitzpeh Nevo in beautiful Ma'ale Adumim, but too many to mention here. You have all been warm and welcoming and made me feel secure and never alone.

Yosef visited for Sukkot about eight weeks after my arrival. He said when he saw me, "You look different, you are different, your neshama is glowing. I am extending the trial period for another year." All I could say was, "Thank you and Baruch Hashem!"

I feel like I have the best of two worlds, one in Israel and one in Ohio with my husband, children and grandchildren. I thank my husband, Yosef, for agreeing to let me do this, as many husbands would not be willing to spend such significant time separated and assume responsibility for the second household. Yosef says before we got married the first time he made a vow to make me the happiest woman in the world. When he was considering my proposal to make aliyah, he said Hashem reminded him of that vow. I go outside every day and thank Hashem for allowing me the privilege of living in Israel. I have to pinch myself every day to make sure it is real.

CHAPTER 23

PARTING THOUGHTS

In the story of Ruth (the quintessential story of conversion), Boaz blesses Ruth with a beautiful bracha, "May the L-rd recompense your efforts; may your reward be complete from the L-rd, the G-d of Israel, under Whose wings you have come to take refuge." And to that we say, "AMEN"! We feel as if our journey is really just beginning.

It seems strange to us that when people ask us why we converted to Judaism, especially religious Jews, and we tell them we were on a search for *emes* and that we seek real intimacy with Hashem, it isn't always a satisfying answer to them. When we explain a little bit of our journey, some understand a little more. But still, I think many people just don't get it. I guess when one is born Jewish, perhaps it's possible to take for granted that your life is built on truth. It is like not understanding the joy of finding something treasured if you have always had it. But for converts, discovering the truth is frightening and exhilarating at the same time, as it completely revolutionizes your relationship with the Creator and Sustainer of the Universe.

We hope by reading this book, Jews by birth can newly appreciate Judaism's traditions and beauties by viewing it through our eyes. We feel so privileged to be a part of this great religion and people. We feel deeply blessed to be part of a Covenant with the Creator and Sustainer of the Universe. How beautiful it is to have come under the wings of the Almighty!

We see our lives and our eventual conversion to Judaism as a beautiful tapestry. It's only when you turn the tapestry over that you see the art, the rich colors, the texture, and the patterns that can make a tapestry a thing of astonishing beauty. Life is a tapestry made of the threads of many experiences, rather than random events with little significance. Our lives had so many unexpected turns. For all Yosef's childhood dreams of playing for the Eagles, the odds of actually playing for the NFL were astronomical. And neither of us ever imagined we would become Torah Jews. There were many turning points, and many significant people.

Our journey has been amazing, and we have so much to be thankful for. Was it an easy journey? Absolutely not – it is most assuredly the hardest thing we ever did. Would we do it all over again? An unequivocal yes. Our prayer that our path would be clear and obvious was answered many times on this journey. Occasionally, we could see a glimpse of what Hashem was weaving into the fabric of our lives. This gave us the courage to keep going, to finish the marathon! This was the advice of Rabbi Bergstein of the Beis Din – it's not a race; it's a marathon! Truly, it was and is a marathon. We are certainly enjoying the journey.

Contact the author at:
ROSEBOWLTORASHI@GMAIL.COM

ACKNOWLEDGMENTS

Many people have been instrumental along our journey. We would like to thank a special group of friends who, when we were still in the process of conversion, made us feel welcome and accepted in the Columbus Jewish community. They opened their homes for many Shabbos and Yom Tov meals and made us feel like we were "part of the tribe." Their encouragement and love made all the difference for us in trying to assimilate into the community and learn the ropes of becoming Torah Jews. They are: Jack and Shelley Levey, Paul and Kathy Pollack, David and Cathy Schwartz, and David Caplan and Ana Echevarria-Morales. Being in the homes of these fine people, observing how to run a kosher kitchen, and many other details of observance have been crucial lessons for us. We are incredibly grateful for your mentorship and friendship. In addition, we would like to acknowledge and thank Rabbi David Claman of Congregation Ahavas Sholom for his excellent teaching and leadership. There are many, many others in the Columbus Jewish Community who welcomed us as well, but far too many to list here. Know that we appreciate and cherish all of you.

Thank you to Rabbi Chaim and Mrs. Chani Capland who opened their homes and hearts to us as soon as we moved into the Jewish community. The weekly parasha and Tanya classes at the Torah Center, as well as many Shabbos and Yom Tov meals, have enhanced our Jewish life, and we value your friendship very much. We know that you are only a phone call away should we be in need of anything at all.

Thank you to Rabbi Areyah and Mrs. Esther Kaltmann who made us feel part of their family and still do. Our first experiences with Shabbos meals were at their home, and they are an example of a family leading a meaningful and vibrant Jewish life. Rabbi Kaltmann represented us to the Beis Din as candidates for conversion, and vouched for our involvement at the shul and the many learning opportunities we embraced. Your love and care for us are appreciated.

Thank you to Rabbi Chaim and Mrs. Menucha Ackerman for agreeing to assume responsibility for the last stages of our conversion. The many meals in your home, advice, friendship, and tutoring helped us immensely, and we are forever grateful. Thank you also for officiating at our chuppah and making it a very special simcha.

Thank you to Yerachmiel Henig and Chayala Levitz, who mentored us throughout our conversion, invited us for Seders, and made us feel like part of their family. Yerachmiel's tutoring on the Laws of Shabbos and other areas of observance prepared us for the various meetings with the Beis Din. We are deeply grateful to both of you.

Yosef would like to thank his chavrusa with whom he studies in the early mornings before Shacharis. They are: Jack Levey, Yaacov Klein, and David Schwartz. Your patience in studying with and teaching me has been a great learning opportunity and one that I treasure. Thank you to Yaacov Gordon who mentored and taught me Hebrew as well as halacha during the weekly Avos U'Banim sessions.

We were fortunate to have made the acquaintance of Mrs. Ahuvah Gray. Being a convert to Judaism herself, she was a wonderful source of advice and encouragement. She has become a dear friend and continues to be an important part of our journey.

Thank you to Rabbi Yakov and Mrs. Judy Goldberg, owners of the Breslov Judaic Center in Columbus. Both of you always showed so much patience and love during our journey when we frequently visited and asked many questions. Your suggestions for seforim to study before and during our conversion were invaluable.

A special thank you to a special friend – April Sharrock. We met at one of the yearly conferences we attended in the Poconos of Pennsylvania. If you're lucky, you meet a person in your life with whom you feel an immediate connection, and that was the case with April. We share special memories of touring Israel twice together. She has been and remains a cherished and true friend.

Thank you to Rabbi Zvi and Mrs. Sara Beth Kahn, who cheered us on every step of the way towards our conversion. They were intensely interested in our progress and were a constant source of encouragement. We enjoyed many happy and delicious Shabbos and Yom Tov meals in their home and were privileged to hear inspirational divrei Torah while at their table.

Thank you to our talented friend and witty editor, Ruti Eastman, without whom this book would not have been possible. She took hundreds of pages of our text and helped us to weave them into a beautiful, coherent and inspirational story. To enjoy some of her musings, see the Appendix for her blog addresses. Also, thank you to Ruti's co-editor and husband, Avi Eastman, aka "Coach," who combed through many pages of football statistics, diligently researching and checking them for accuracy, as well as reading the entire manuscript, making thoughtful suggestions to help make the football part of the story come to life.

Thank you to our friend and innovative graphic designer, Morgan Lael, who designed the interior of the book, created visually appealing covers for the book, and used her tech-savvy knowledge to handle the self-publishing part of this project.

We are grateful to several people who sacrificed their time in reading the draft manuscript, making corrections, suggestions and serving as extra pairs of eyes to, hopefully, make this book an encouragement and inspiration to others: Dr. David Caplan, Dr. Ana Echevarria-Morales, Rabbi Chaim Capland, Chaya Bluma Hadar, Ovadia Tolbert, Adina Mishkoff Kischel, and Hannah Murray. A special thank you to my amazing and talented sister, Elisa, for helping me polish the manuscript and make this book the best that it could be.

Thank you to Dr. Larry and Mrs. Meryl Weprin, the couple who initially encouraged us to chronicle our journey in book form. Thank you, Meryl, for suggesting the title of the book.

A big shout out to our awesome children: Cal, Jr., Brandon, Andrew, Corey, Isaiah, and Hannah. They are the ones most intimately involved in our journey and the ones who had to bear the brunt of the numerous changes to our household, not the least of which was adhering to a kosher kitchen, adapting to our Shabbat schedule, giving up some of their favorite family meals, and a myriad of other major changes at home and elsewhere. We understand what a sacrifice it has been for you. We love you and appreciate your patience and understanding.

Finally, and most importantly, thank you to HaKadosh Baruch Hu (the Holy One, Blessed Be He), who guides our lives with light, love and holiness every single second of every single day.

REFLECTIONS FROM OUR CHILDREN

CALVIN, JR.

Let me start by saying that my family has always been religious and has tried to abide by the Ten Commandments and the non-denominational Christian faith ever since I was born. When my dad and step-mom came together roughly 25 years ago, I believe their journey to find their truth began. As kids we were always questioning some of the information we were being given. We had a difficult time with ideas of the rapture, burning in hell and being separated from G-d, and always feeling like we were living under this microscope. If G-d is all knowing, then wouldn't he have already pre-selected individuals to enter into heaven? It wouldn't matter what we did on earth because G-d would already know who is going to make it and who isn't. That did not sound fair to us, nor did the idea of burning in a fiery pit for eternity. Maybe this was the spark that started them on their journey.

Having said that, I believe that there is a G-d that loves us and cares about us dearly. G-d wants the best for us and wants us to be happy and enjoy life, not live under a microscope in fear that we will be struck down, not in fear of making mistakes and constantly looking over your shoulder. There is a reason the windshield on a car is larger than the rear-view mirror. It's more important where you're going than where you have been. Although the past shapes and molds us to who we are, past experiences are like a reflection on a glass ball. It's important to see those experiences but also to look through them to see the lessons, either good or bad.

Therefore, I do like some of the ideas or beliefs that are presented in the Jewish faith. I feel that my parents are happier, healthier, and more fulfilled. I believe it saved my dad's life, since he had to change his eating habits to being kosher. No more sneaking to Bob Evans or McDonalds. I also like the fact that we should not fear death; rather, it is the next step in our spiritual journey.

There are some adjustments that we have made that don't always work out in our favor. First, we live four hours from Columbus. Whenever we come into town, we have to try to make arrangements on Sunday instead of Saturday and this can make for a short visit because we have to drive back home. Second, we love to go out to eat when we visit. That can be rather difficult, since there are not a whole lot of options that we can choose from that my kids would eat. Lastly, the name changes: I understand that this is part of the religion, but I feel that G-d gave us the names we were supposed to have when we were born. If not, then does that mean that G-d makes mistakes? I don't think that's the case, but I'm just reflecting on the changes that have been different for us to adjust to. Because of the changes they have made, it has caused us kids to question our faith and what we were taught. This has been the biggest dividing factor in our family, as some of the family members feel that the practices they have incorporated are rather extreme. We have always felt that religion should not interfere with your daily life, but run parallel to it.

Additionally, my two biggest concerns are that on Saturday or Shabbos, we cannot get ahold of them via phone and that can be frustrating. If there is an emergency it's difficult to contact them. And what about when my kids get older and are involved in sports or other events on Saturdays? Will they be able to take part in coming to see them participate? I am a former college and NFL running back like my dad. My collegiate games were on Saturdays and my dad was always in the stands at home and away games. It was very important to have my parents and grandparents in the stands supporting me. How will I explain to my kids that their grandparents cannot attend because they are not allowed to drive to their events?

In closing, I believe we each find G-d in our own ways. How we connect with the creator is unique to all of us. Enjoy life, smile, have fun with the world that was created for our enjoyment. See the beauty in what G-d has created, from the details in a flower, in how it opens every morning to let the sunlight in, to the depths of the ocean, or how life is created between a couple and our amazing human body in all its unique features. I am happy that my parents have found what they believe is truth and makes them happy, and how they feel like they've connected with the creator in the unique way that G-d has instilled in them.

BRANDON

It was hardly surprising when my parents decided to de-convert from Christianity entirely after taking part in Messianic Judaism for a number of years. I had witnessed their journey every step of the way—the countless hours of studying, reflection, and soul searching—and it was hard to find fault with its conclusion. In fact, I came to the same conclusion on Christianity shortly after their de-conversion.

Although I understood their de-conversion, there was no way I, or any of my siblings, could have appreciated how different Orthodox Judaism is from Christianity or, even, Messianic Judaism. Messianic Judaism essentially just changed which day of the week they went to church, and which holidays we celebrated as a family; Orthodox Judaism is an all-encompassing way of life.

If I'm being honest (and that's the point of this), Orthodox Judaism was a step in the wrong direction for my parents, and not just because of how it has impacted our lives with arbitrary formalities and rules. Growing up as Christians, the biblical god's behavior was somewhat excused, because Jesus was said to represent a new covenant. But now that the Torah is their only holy book, there is no softening the atrocities commanded and committed by the biblical god all throughout. The worst part to me, however, is that belief in the Torah requires one to reject some of the most profound scientific facts discovered over the last 2000 years, facts that literally change one's perspective on reality.

And that's not at all to imply that Orthodox Jews are bad people or anything of the sort. Through association with my parents I have had the pleasure to congregate with many over the years and I couldn't have been treated any kinder. When I was considering converting to Judaism myself, quite a few rabbis took time out of their busy schedules to meet with me and answer my questions. I was always impressed with how genuinely nice they all were. Furthermore, my parents have never been treated better by a group of people, nor had the close friendships that they do now. It's no wonder they're drawn in by the sense of community that Orthodox Judaism provides.

I am thankful for my parents' journey because I don't think I would have had mine otherwise. Growing up, I had so many questions about the Bible's discrepancies, etc., but I put them to the side because I was scared to "question God". But I was never at ease. My parents' conversion inspired me to examine my beliefs critically for the first time, to not just believe something because I was indoctrinated from a young age. So for years I studied the Bible (and Torah), how it came to be, who its authors were, the cultures that inspired it, and how its claims stack up to what we now know. I went from a fundamentalist Christian, to a would-be Jewish convert (not Orthodox, I knew I wouldn't have the discipline for that), to an atheist. Along the way I discovered my love for science and I have clarity, finally. I owe that to my parents and I'm incredibly thankful.

I'm also incredibly thankful to my parents for how they raised us. As you can tell from some of our reflections, there was a little resentment when they first converted, because we were essentially told that we had been living a lie. But they did the best they could given what they knew, and their love for us has always been apparent. Despite shaking up our worldview, we are all incredibly lucky to have been raised the way we were and to have had the childhoods we did. My parents are the most selfless and dedicated people I know, and although I don't agree with their views, I have immense respect for their dedication. In a way, I am happy that they are happy, but it's not so simple for me. I love them so much and I worry what will happen if their foundation is shaken again, with more invested this time. It's true that I've never seen them happier and more fulfilled; only time will tell if that's for the best.

ANDREW (AND SON JUDAH)

I have come to respect Judaism as a lifestyle, as opposed to religious doctrine. The only reason I could have reached this level of respect can be firmly and exclusively attributed to my parents. From childhood, we were involved in non-denominational Christianity, which may have caused spiritual confusion among my siblings as we got older. Though the change from Christianity to Orthodox Judaism from a religious perspective may sound severe; well, it's because the change is most definitely severe.

I refuse to cast a negative light on Christianity, but I will address the positive changes I have noticed in both parents' lives since converting to Orthodox Judaism. Most importantly, the diet restrictions (changing over from non-kosher to kosher) have performed wonders in my parents' lives, especially my father's. If he had not converted to Judaism, his life may have been shortened significantly because he was eating fast food, which he cannot do anymore, since he lives in Columbus and there are no kosher establishments. It's incredible to see the visible changes in my dad's health. I believe my father would still be eating at McDonald's and Bob Evans had he not converted (Sorry, Dad).

I do want to make something perfectly clear: I completely support my parents in everything in regards to Judaism. At no point during their conversion, or any time after, have they forced their lifestyle down our throats. My son, Kingston Judah Murray, is Jewish by blood. He loves learning about his Jewish side every time he is with my parents and demands Bubbe (Emunah) bring him to Israel!! There's clearly something special about the Jewish people. For this reason, I can say I have seen the difference between a "religion" and a commitment to a new life, for which they are most proud. I secretly wish I could be a part of the club, but I don't think I possess the discipline to avoid snacks (non-kosher). But I digress. I apologize for being long-winded, but I am very proud to have my parents and to watch their progression through something so rigorous and very much worth every step. I love you two!! Shabbat Shalom!! (Did I say that right?)

COREY

I'm happy that my parents are happy.

ISAIAH

Although I completely disagree with my parents' religious choice, and any religion for that matter, I'm happy that they have found fulfillment in their choice.

HANNAH

My parents' conversion was not easy on our family. There was confusion and resentment from some in our family. It was especially hard on my own faith. Going from being a staunch Christian to an Orthodox Jew shattered everything that I believed. At first, I felt lost, but then I realized that I needed to discover what I believed in for myself. I needed to stop basing my beliefs on what my parents did, but figure things out on my own. At that point it became freeing, knowing that what I believed was my choice. I am still on a journey to figure out what that is, but seeing my parents figure it out for themselves gives me hope. My parents are truly an inspiration. They did not become complacent in their beliefs, but strived for truth. I respect my parents immensely for their passion and dedication to what they believe. I have incredible role models of what it looks like to go after something with your whole heart and work hard for it every single day.

CALVIN MURRAY FOOTBALL STATISTICS

HIGH SCHOOL STATS:

- Outstanding scholar athlete
- Nine varsity letters, 3 in football, 3 in basketball, 1 in baseball and 2 in track and field
- First Team All-South Jersey 1976
- All Conferences 1975 and 1976
- South Jersey Player of the Week September 1975
- All-Area 1975 and 1976
- High School American 1976
- Inducted Millville Sports Hall of Fame 2006

THE OHIO STATE UNIVERSITY BUCKEYES STATS:

- Full football scholarship
- Four varsity letters as running back
  - Named All Big 10 First Team 1980
  - Honorable Mention All-American 1980
  - Big 10 Rushing Champ 1980
  - Chevrolet Player of the Game 1980 vs. UCLA
  - Ohio State Most Valuable Player 1980
  - Co-Captain of 1980 team
- Played Sugar Bowl, Gator Bowl, Rose Bowl and Fiesta Bowl as well as Japan Bowl for College All-stars

THIRTEEN ARTICLES OF FAITH
(MOSES MAIMONIDES 1135-1204)

1. Belief in the existence of G-d.

2. Belief in G-d's unity.

3. Belief in G-d's incorporeality.

4. Belief in G-d's eternity.

5. Belief that G-d alone is to be worshipped.

6. Belief in prophecy.

7. Belief in Moses as the greatest of the prophets.

8. Belief that the Torah was given by G-d to Moses.

9. Belief that the Torah is immutable.

10. Belief that G-d knows the thoughts and deeds of men.

11. Belief that G-d rewards and punishes.

12. Belief in the advent of the Messiah.

13. Belief in the resurrection of the dead.

GLOSSARY

Note: Throughout the book, you will see different spellings for transliterations for some words, such as "Shabbos" and "Shabbat," which both mean "the Sabbath," or "kashrus" and "kashrut," different pronunciations for the word for the kosher dietary laws. We decided to allow for these differences, as they illustrated our passage from living in the American Jewish community to spending more time in Israel, and because different organizations prefer different transliteration. We hope that you will not be inconvenienced by this decision, as you "travel with us" on our journey.

Aliyah, aliyot (pl) – "ascent," "the act of going up," receiving an aliyah to the Torah; the honor of reciting the blessing over the Torah; immigration to Israel

Am Yisrael – The People (Nation) of Israel

Ari Mikveh – the ritual bath used by The Arizal, Isaac Luria, located in Tsfat (Safed), in northern Israel

Arutz Sheva – Channel 7; an online radio station in Israel

Avos u'banim – fathers and sons (parents and children)

Baal Shem Tov – Rabbi Yisroel ben Eliezer, commonly known as the Baal Shem Tov, a mystical rabbi, and considered the founder of Hasidic Judaism

Bashert – one's intended or "soulmate," often seen as decreed in Heaven before birth

Beis Din (Beit Din) – house of judgment; a rabbinical court of Judaism

Beit Lechem – Bethlehem

Bimah - raised platform in the synagogue from which the Torah is read

Binah - understanding

Birkat Hamazon – Grace after Meals

Birkat Kohanim – the priestly blessing, delivered daily in Israeli synagogues and at other special occasions by all kohanim present

Bitachon – generally translated as "trust"

Bracha – blessing (plural brachot or brachos)

Bris (brit) milah – Covenant of Circumcision

Challah – special braided bread eaten on Sabbath and Jewish holidays

Chazak – strong; be strong

Chochmah – wisdom

Chosson – groom

Chumash – Five Books of Moses

Chuppah – lit. "canopy" or "covering," a canopy under which a Jewish couple stand during their Jewish wedding ceremony

Da'at - knowledge

Davening – praying

Devarim – fifth book of the Hebrew Bible
(corresponds to Deuteronomy)

Emes (emet) – usually translated as "truth"

Emunah – Biblical faith

Esrog – yellow citron used during the week-long holiday
of Succos, as one of the four species

Ger – convert to Judaism

Geirus (gerus or geirut) – Conversion to Judaism

G-d – according to Jewish law, the various names for our Creator
are all considered to be holy, and must be treated with the utmost
respect. Therefore, we write this name with the "o" replaced by
a hyphen, as a sign of respect

Hatafat dam brit - ritual extraction of a drop of blood

Haftorah – a short reading from the Prophets that follows
the reading from the Chumash in a synagogue

Hakadosh Baruch Hu – The Holy One, Blessed Be He

Halacha – Jewish religious laws derived from the Written and

Oral Torah; according to Jewish law

Hanukkah – Jewish festival, lasting eight days from the 25th day of Kislev, commemorating the rededication of the Temple in 165 BC by the Maccabees after its desecration by the Syrians

Hashem – literally "the name" – used to refer to G-d, thus avoiding G-d's more formal title (as a sign of respect)

Hashgacha Pratis (pratit) – Divine providence

Hasidic/Hasidut (also sometimes Chassidic/Chassidus) – relating to a specific Jewish religious group oriented in part toward a mystical (as opposed to rigorously academic) approach

Havdalah – brief ceremony marking the end of the Shabbat

Hitbodedut - personal communication with G-d, a very Jewish kind of meditation

Kabbalah – mystical interpretation of the Bible

Kabbalat Shabbat – Friday evening service at the synagogue that welcomes the Sabbath with songs and psalms

Kallah – bride

Kashrus(kashrut) – laws concerning permitted/forbidden foods

Kedusha – holiness

Kesubah (Ketubah) – a Jewish marriage contract outlining the rights and responsibilities of the groom in relation to the bride

Kiddush Hashem – sanctification of G-d's name

Kippahs (also Kipot) – another word for yarmulke or skullcap, a cloth head covering worn by Jewish men

Kittel – a white cotton or linen robe worn by Orthodox Jewish men at the Passover Seder, on Rosh Hashana, on Yom Kippur, and used as a burial shroud

Kever – grave

Kiddush – sanctification; blessing recited over wine or grape juice to sanctify the Shabbat and Jewish holiday; also, the communal gathering after the Sabbath or holiday morning services

Ki Tisa – Hebrew for "when you take," is the 21st weekly Torah portion in the annual Jewish cycle of Torah reading

Kohanim - priests

Kol hakavod – Well done!

Kotel – a remnant of the retaining wall from the Second Temple in Jerusalem

Lech Lecha – Hebrew for "go!" or "leave!", literally "go for you" is the third weekly Torah portion in the annual Jewish cycle of Torah reading

Lulav – frond of the date palm tree; one of the Four Species used during the holiday of Succos

Machpelah – "double tomb"; the cave which Abraham bought, together with the field in which it stood, from Ephron the Hittite, for a family burying-place

Maariv – Jewish prayer service held in the evening or night

Mechitzah – partition used to separate men and women, usually during prayer

Mezuzah/Mezuzot – a parchment inscribed with specific versus from the Torah and attached in a case to the doorpost of a Jewish house

Midrash – commentary on the Biblical text

Mikveh – a bath used for ritual immersion in Judaism

Mincha – afternoon prayer service

Minyan - a quorum of ten men over the age of 13 required for traditional Jewish public worship

Mitzvah/Mitzvot (also mitzvahs or mitzvos)– commandment(s); good deed(s) done from religious duty

Mohel – ritual circumcisor

Motzei Shabbos – the time in the evening immediately following the Sabbath

Neshama - soul

Noahide Laws – the seven laws given to Noah after the Flood, which decree the establishment of a fair system of justice in society, and prohibit idolatry, blasphemy, murder, adultery and incest, robbery, and the eating of flesh taken from a living animal

Olim – immigrants to Israel

Orthodox Judaism – Judaism that observes the Torah and Talmud through strict observance of the Sabbath, religious festivals, holy days, and the dietary laws

Parnassa – livelihood; income; ability to earn a living

Parasha – portion, the weekly Torah portion in Hebrew

Pesach – Passover, a Jewish festival commemorating the liberation by G-d from slavery in Egypt

Pesach Seder - feast that includes reading, drinking wine, telling stories, eating special foods and singing, commemorating the anniversary of our nation's miraculous exodus from Egyptian slavery more than 3,000 years ago

Purim – Jewish festival commemorating the defeat of Haman's plot to massacre the Jews as chronicled in the book of Esther

Rashi – Shlomo Yitzchaki, generally known by the acronym Rashi, was a medieval French rabbi and author of a comprehensive commentary on the Talmud and commentary on the Tanakh

Rochel Imeinu – "Rachel our mother"; the favorite of Biblical patriarch Jacob's two wives as well as the mother of Joseph and Benjamin, two of the twelve progenitors of the tribes of Israel

Rosh Hashanah – the Jewish New Year

Seder – retelling of the story of liberation of the Israelites from slavery in ancient Egypt accompanied by a festive meal

Shabbos/Shabbat – Jewish Sabbath

Shabbos Kallah - a gathering of women to offer blessings and good tidings to the bride, on the Shabbos before the wedding

Shacharis – daily morning prayer

Sheitel – wig (Yiddish)

Shavuos (also Shavuot) – festival commemorating the giving of the Torah on Mt. Sinai

Shiurim (pl) – lessons on Torah topics

Shomeret – mikveh attendant

Shuk –Arabic for marketplace; in Jerusalem, refers usually to Mahane Yehuda, the world-famous vegetable and fruit market that has grown to be an open-air shopping mall with restaurants

Shul – Yiddish word for synagogue

Shulchan Aruch – Code of Jewish Law

Siddur – Jewish prayer book

Simcha – lit. happiness; often refers to a family celebration, such as a wedding or other life-cycle event

Succah – a temporary shelter covered in natural materials, used especially for meals during the Jewish festival of Succos

Succos (Sukkot) – Feast of Booths, commonly translated to English as Feast of Tabernacles

Tallis (tallit) – fringed shawl worn by Jewish men at prayer

Talmud – body of Jewish civil and ceremonial law and legend comprising the Mishnah and the Gemara

Tanakh (Tanach) – the Hebrew Bible, acronym for Torah, Nevi'im (Prophets) and Ketuvin (Writings), consisting of 24 books

Tanya – writings of Hasidic philosophy, by Rabbi Shneur Zalman of Liadi, the founder of Chabad Hasidism

Tzitzis (tzitit) – fringes attached to a tallis. According to the Torah, the purpose of wearing tzitzis is to serve as a reminder to Jews of their religious obligations

Yad Hashem – hand of Hashem

Yahrzeit - the anniversary of someone's death, especially a parent

Yichud – seclusion

Yiddishkeit – Jewish way of life

Yom Kippur – holiest day of the year in Judaism; also known of as the Day of Atonement

Yom Tov – lit "good day"; used in reference to a Jewish festival, especially Pesach, Shavuos, Rosh Hashanah or Succos

APPENDIX

Listed below are some movies, books and websites we like.

WEBSITES:

Fromrosebowltorashi.com
Many articles, radio interviews, YouTube clips, newspaper articles, photos, and speaking engagements locations and dates can be found here.

- Alephbeta.org
- Aish.com
- Chabad.org
- Simpletoremember.com
- Outreachjudaism.org
  Rabbi Tovia Singer's site
- Lazerbrody.typepad.com
  Rabbi Lazer Brody's site
- Templeinstitute.org
- Ruti Eastman's blogs: rutieastman.blogspot.com
  rutimizrachi.blogspot.com
- Emunah's blog: mybeautifulaliyah.com
- Wrapunzel.com
  Beautiful ways to cover your hair; one of Emunah's favorite websites!
- Tenfromthenations.com

MOVIES:

Leap of Faith | *Searching for truth and meaning in their lives, this group of unlikely Americans takes a leap of faith and undergo conversion from Christianity to Orthodox Judaism.* Ruthfilms.com

BOOKS:

Adler, Rivkah Lambert | *Ten From The Nations: Torah Awakening Among Non-Jews*

Arush, Shalom | *Garden of Emunah, Garden of Wisdom, Garden of Riches, Garden of Education, Universal Garden of Emunah, Trail to Tranquility, Women's Wisdom, In Forest Fields, Garden of Healing, Garden of Gratitude, Garden of Peace*

Ashear David | *Living Emunah*

Eastman, Ruti | *From Big Whine to Big Grapes: A Collection of Essays on Aliyah and Life in Israel, as Seen Through Rosé-Filled Glasses*

Gray, Ahuvah | *In Search of Hidden Treasures, Journey to the Land of my Soul, Gifts of a Stranger,* and *My Sister the Jew*

Jacobson, Simon | *Toward a Meaningful Life*

Jungreis, Esther | *The Committed Life*

Kitov, Eliyahu | *The Book of Our Heritage: The Jewish Year and Its Days of Significance*

Norman, Asher | *26 Reasons Why Jews Don't Believe in Jesus*

Samson, David | *Torat Eretz Yisrael – The Teachings of HaRav Tzvi Yehuda HaCohen Kook, Lights On Orot*

Singer, Tovia | *Let's Get Biblical*

Teichtal, Yisachar Shlomo | *Eim Habanim Semeichah: On Eretz Yisrael, Redemption, and Unity*

Made in the USA
Middletown, DE
12 April 2018